D1208488

COPS ON CAMPUS AND
CRIME IN THE STREETS

Erle Stanley Gardner

COPS
ON CAMPUS
AND
CRIME
IN THE STREETS

William Morrow and Company, Inc., New York

19 70

Contents

COPS ON CAMPUS AND
CRIME IN THE STREETS

1   Handcuffing Police

A TELEVISION store in a California city had been plagued by repeated burglaries.

It was situated in a highly vulnerable position. A building, which was vacant at night, was on each side of the store. There was a parking space where a driver could run a car around to the back, and a similar parking place where a car or cars could be parked by the front of the store.

After several break-ins, police asked the neighbors in a nearby two-story flat to notify them if they saw anything suspicious.

One night one of the neighbors saw a car and covered trailer move up to the television store and park.

The neighbor immediately telephoned the police, stating that he thought it was a suspicious circumstance and that the people in the car might be intending to load the trailer with television sets, radios, and tape recorders.

The police promised to be right out.

They never got there.

The next day one of the police officers hunted up the person who had done the telephoning.

"I'm sorry," he said. "We were all prepared to come out when we received word of a student riot on the grounds of the high school. We, all of us, had to rush out there and stand in line to hold the kids back."

This is illustrative of a stark fact that is not widely understood at the present time—there are not enough police to give us adequate protection against crime.

Of late we have been piling extra duties upon our police, duties which are not only time-consuming but which tend to make the criminals bolder and undermine the respect which the community should have for its police force.

In addition to that, what with recent decisions of the Supreme Court protecting the rights of persons accused of crime, the duties of the police have become far more complicated.

There are two ways of looking at these decisions. Some people think they will be beneficial in the long run. Others feel that they have taken the handcuffs off the wrists of the criminals and put them on the wrists of the police. Whichever way you look at it, the decisions have added greatly to the duties of the police and complicated the problem of crime investigation.

Take for instance a case with which I was familiar, the case of a widow living alone in a fairly large house in a respectable neighborhood.

There was a young man living a few doors down the street. Sometimes when she saw him walking home she would give him a ride. On one of these occasions he showed signs of distress and asked if he could use her bathroom. She thought nothing of it and unlocked the door of her house, told him where the bathroom was, and went into the kitchen to busy herself with some dishes in the sink.

Something, perhaps a noise, perhaps some extrasensory perception, suddenly caused her to turn.

The man was stalking her with outstretched hands. He

grabbed her, choked her, and tried to twist the string of her apron around her throat. She fought as best she could, but was losing the battle when a third person entered the house, whereupon the man ran out and disappeared.

No one heard anything of him for more than three years. Then he was apprehended.

When the police told him he was under arrest he didn't deny the charge.

The police brought this young man back for trial.

The district attorney wouldn't touch the case with a ten-foot pole.

The prosecution went into court and moved to dismiss the case. The judge was forced to grant the motion with extreme reluctance.

Any statements the man had made were made before he had been advised of his rights. Apparently he was not told that he need not say anything, but if he did say anything his statements could be used against him; that he was entitled to an attorney in every stage of the proceedings. This is the formula which must now be recited to a suspect at the time of arrest, according to the Supreme Court decision in the Miranda case.

Furthermore, the defendant had been absent for three years, and in California there is a statute of limitations under which nearly all felonies can not be prosecuted after three years.

The man was dismissed from court, went back to his home, and started living his usual life, walking back and forth past the house of the woman he had attacked.

A psychologist who was attending court and studying the man (the woman believes this was done at the request of the trial judge) came to her and said, "This man is dangerous. He has the temperament that will cause him to repeat this crime at some favorable opportunity. He is a deadly menace to society."

"What would you suggest that I do?" the woman asked.

"There's only one thing to do," the psychologist told her. "Sell your house, change your name, move to some other city, and don't leave any back trail. Otherwise this man is going to get you sooner or later."

The woman, who had lived in that city for most of her life and had a host of friends there, rebelled at following the advice and decided to brave it out. But she is now living under a daily strain.

This story illustrates one aspect of the changing situation which is developing in criminal law.

In this case the victim was advised to become the fugitive, while the culprit triumphantly returned to his abode and resumed life just as he left it.

Criminals are not exactly dumb. They make use of all the advantages which are placed at their disposal. In addition to new technical advantages of the law as described above they use technological gains. Among these is that of rapid transportation.

The criminals now have a *modus operandi* where the persons who use it are known as "minute men."

Take for instance the television and radio store which I commented about earlier. It installed an elaborate burglar alarm system.

That didn't do any good. The "minute men" figured that they had a maximum of three minutes after the alarm went off before the police could pick up the alarm, transmit it over the police transmittal system to a radio car and have the radio car get on the job.

So a closed panel truck, not once, but several times, would pull up in front of the television store. The thieves would come rushing out and use cement blocks to smash in the show window. Then they would start grabbing everything they could get hold of and transport it to the waiting truck, where the driver sat with his eyes on a stopwatch.

At the end of so many seconds the driver would give a signal. The men would scramble out of the store pell-mell into the pickup. The doors would swing shut and the looters would be gone long before the frustrated police arrived on the scene.

This finally got to be too much for the owner of the television store. He moved to another location where he felt he would have more protection and where he would be less vulnerable to the raids of the "minute men."

Once again the victim had to be the one to run away, leaving the criminals at large.

These stories reveal only one small aspect of what is going on today as evidence that police protection is no longer adequate against crimes which menace the average citizen.

Moreover, crimes are now taking a particularly vicious twist. Today's criminal is often a sadistic individual who thinks nothing of beating up his victim when the loot isn't sufficient to suit him, or shooting the victim in cold blood just so the person won't be able to identify him later on.

Even so, the criminals of today haven't as yet discovered how really inadequate police protection has become. They are, however, learning rapidly, as witness the number of vicious crimes which are committed on the streets of our cities, crimes which in many instances are so numerous that the newspapers have grown tired of reporting them and lump them into a few paragraphs of statistics.

For example, here is a news article from *The New York Times* of Sunday, July 6, 1969. I quote it in its entirety.

Study Finds Police Forces Below Quota in Big Cities

Washington, July 5 (UPI)—A survey has disclosed that the average police force in the nation's largest cities was 10 percent below its quota in 1967, the President's Commission on Law Enforcement and Administration of Justice reported today.

The average police force in 1967 for all cities, the survey said, had a deficit of 5 percent. This occurred despite an increase in population and a crime rate rise of 89 percent from 1960 to 1968, it said.

What is just as startling as the statistics in this article is the fact that these figures didn't make headlines. Quite the opposite! The average edition of the Sunday *New York Times* contains thousands of words. This story of less than one hundred words was "buried" on page 25 of the second section.

But we don't really need the President's Commission on Law Enforcement to tell us that police forces are understaffed, cops overworked, and that crime is on the increase. A reading of the day's events themselves in the newspaper or our own experiences makes it obvious that we don't have enough police. It is equally obvious that by placing too many new duties on the police, such as we already have, we are handcuffing law enforcement.

I believe we must act now to take the handcuffs off our cops and thereby help our police function more efficiently.

2   Supporting Police

THERE ARE certain things the police must have in order to function efficiently.

They must have adequate personnel.

They must have mobility—although this is really a component of personnel, because by mobility the police can get along with less personnel than otherwise would be the case.

They must have time to complete their investigations.

They must have freedom from political interference and, above all, they must have public support and understanding.

It needs only a glance at any daily newspaper to realize the frightening extent to which we are undermining the efficiency of the police.

The nation's police did not have adequate personnel prior to our putting cops on the campus.

When we take officers out of radio patrol cars to keep the campuses open we make matters worse by rendering the police static instead of mobile. In order to function efficiently the force has to be highly mobile. Police today are being deprived of mobility.

Once the police get into "confrontations" with students or others the whole political situation enters the picture.

continue his career of breaking into stores and getting television sets and tape recorders.

Moreover, John Doe has friends. They see him lounging around the night spots, being a big shot with the dolls, and wonder where he is getting all the money. When they find out, they are very apt to decide that this is a lucrative field and they'd better get in on it while the getting is good.

So we have John Doe committing a lot of crimes and his friends joining the ranks of the criminals.

If the police are sufficiently numerous and efficient so John Doe can be captured and put away for a long time, it not only puts a stop to his activities but those of other people who might be tempted by John Doe's success and who are deterred by his failure.

This is one of the reasons that it is so difficult to tell anything about crime statistics.

It is not only the number of crimes which counts but it is the number of professional criminals who are making their living out of crime that is significant. In looking only at statistics we can't really tell whether a lot more people are committing a few crimes each or a relatively few people are committing many more crimes.

There is, however, one infallible way of measuring crime. When it becomes unsafe for the law-abiding citizen to walk the street at night we can assume not only that is crime on the increase but that the number of criminals is growing. Then it has reached such a point society must take drastic steps if it is to survive.

That time is now.

The first step is to have a better understanding of police problems and of police work. We must do the things which improve police efficiency and cease to do the things which impair it.

For the past thirty years I have been interested in homicide investigation and in police science. Some twenty-two years ago I helped organize the so-called Court of Last Resort and from my experience with that organization learned a lot about the investigation of crime.

Ever since that time I have been in intimate contact with police, with prison inmates, wardens, and investigators. Because I have had a peculiar unofficial status I have had an opportunity to gather information that might otherwise have been denied.

Many a prison inmate has confided in me as he would a "buddy." Wardens have not only told me intimate stories of prison life, but one of them went so far as to keep a tape recorder in his office and send me tapes of convict interviews when he thought I would be interested.

I have been given many honors by police. I am an Honorary Texas Ranger with the rank of captain. I am a deputy in several counties in Texas. The city trustees of Wichita, Kansas, appointed me an honorary chief of police of Wichita. I am a life member of the Kansas Peace Officers' Association. I am one of the one hundred Gold Star Deputies of Alameda County, California, and a deputy sheriff of Butte and Riverside counties in California. I have a diamond-studded star presented to me by the Texas Sheriff's Association. I am an honorary member of the Fraternal Order of Police. I have spent a great deal of time patrolling with officers in radio cars. I have twice attended Captain Frances G. Lee's seminars in homicide investigation at Harvard University. I am an honorary lifetime member of the American Polygraph Association, and I have a backlog of twenty-five years' courtroom experience as a trial lawyer.

I have had enough experience to feel certain that we are not appreciating the problems which have been presented to us by the developments of the past few years. I don't think we understand the inevitable results of what will happen in the months and years to come unless we take control with a firm hand and see that disturbances on the campuses are not quelled at the expense of murders in the home and crime on the streets.

In addition to adequate numbers of officers the police need mobility.

I well remember some years ago when I was surprised to see a map in the office of the chief of police of a fairly large city showing a time sequence by means of pins with various-colored heads.

The chief was using this chart or map in order to arrange a daily shifting of forces.

It was interesting to see how life pulsed and throbbed in this big city and how this affected police problems.

Most people went to work in the morning. From seven-thirty to eight-thirty the traffic was heavy on the principal thoroughfares leading to the business district. Toward eight-thirty the police had to be on the lookout for people who had a late start, who had to be at the office at nine o'clock, who were speeding and taking chances on traffic lights in order to get there.

After nine things quieted down for a while; then came the lunch hour with its special traffic problems for the police.

Then the schools let out, and there was a safety problem. About five o'clock the flow of traffic from the business district to the residential district commenced. In an hour or two came the businessmen who had stopped at cocktail lounges to have a quick one or two before dinner, who had met other businessmen with whom they wanted to talk, who had suddenly looked at their watches and realized how late the hour was. This type of driver would start in a hurry, with a little alcohol affecting his judgment and a burning desire to get home before dinner guests arrived or before his irate wife had cause to berate him for delaying dinner.

These people presented a definite difficulty for the police.

Then later on there would be the problems of nightclubs, of the theatrical district; of mugging down in the dark alleys and the situations which arose along skid row.

The police chief didn't have enough personnel to cope with all of these problems, therefore he had to shift his personnel. Officers would be on duty in a certain precinct at certain hours, then they would shift to other precincts. And so the city was adequately protected by keeping the police officers shifting around with a high degree of mobility and an understanding of the difficulties of the city.

Now then, suppose citizens suddenly add a tremendous burden to the duties of the police? Suppose a number of police are rushed to a high school or college, not simply to make arrests but to stand there as human targets for insults and projectiles?

The average citizen on one of the main thoroughfares will now be in far more danger of being clobbered by a drunk driver who has stayed too long at a cocktail lounge. The person who is on the fringes of skid row will now be more apt to be mugged. Houses in high-class residential districts are far more apt to be burglarized during that period of the evening when people are out to dinner and a movie, thus leaving their houses unprotected.

Society can't eat its cake and have it too. And the police officer can't be in two places at once.

Moreover, remember again that every unsolved crime is cumulative in its effect. It means the perpetrator of that crime is still at large, committing more crimes, and it means that his success in getting away with his illegal activities is a form of encouragement to other criminals.

In addition to mobility the police need time.

There are some crimes which can't be solved on the spot. The solution takes time, often a lot of time.

I remember some years ago when I was familiar with a series of crimes in Honolulu.

These crimes puzzled the police because they felt certain they were being committed by one man because of the so-called *modus operandi*.

The police worked on the case with dogged persistence, but houses continued to be burglarized. For a while the crimes would be in one district; then they would be in another district. Police records showed that at first the crimes would all be between the same hours, then suddenly the hours would shift to another segment of time, and then they would shift back again.

The police worked on that case literally for months, and then, because of the dogged persistence of their investigation, some bright individual in the police department discovered that the shift in the time element coincided exactly with the shift in the time element of the changeover in taxi drivers.

So the police came to the conclusion that the man who was perpetrating the crimes was a taxi driver.

From then on it was all downhill. Within a short period they had the man they wanted and had recovered large quantities of loot.

Here was a good illustration of one man who was committing crime after crime after crime. He was responsible for a staggering number of burglaries.

Sometimes the police have red-hot clues to work on, and at other times they have to track down hundreds of cold leads. They need time to do this.

I recall one case in a Western city where the police were working on a crime which in turn tied in with a whole series of other cases. The only clue the police had as to the perpetrator of the crimes was a hat which had been dropped at the scene of the most recent crime.

This was a city of over a hundred and fifty thousand inhabitants, a highly complex city with an agricultural as well as a metropolitan background.

All the police had was a battered, worn hat. There were no distinguishing marks by which the original sale of the article could be traced. It was a slouch hat whose soft brim had been tugged this way and that, giving it an individuality of its own, something which perhaps was an index to the character of the man who owned it.

The detectives who studied the hat came to the conclusion that it was one belonging to a minority group of itinerant farm workers. They knew that the latter are likely to be gregarious and in the habit of congregating in certain pool halls and beer parlors.

Since the crime was one of a series which the police wanted very much to solve they went all out on the case. They prepared a dummy head on which they put the hat. They knew that persons in the income group which they were investigating were inclined toward certain hangouts. So, painstakingly, one by one, the police covered these various places and they drew a blank.

Then the police shifted their activities to neighboring cities, smaller communities, where agricultural workers gathered.

Finally, in a community several miles away from the city, the police got a lead. A witness thought the head with the hat on it looked "something like" a certain individual.

The police went to work collecting data on the background of this individual, trying to find out his whereabouts at the time the crimes in question had been committed and particularly at the time the latest one had been perpetrated. They put an unobtrusive shadow on the suspect and, eventually, gathered enough information to enable them to make an arrest.

The point is that this is patient, dogged investigative work which requires a lot of time. If the police don't have the time to put in, they can't do this type of work. If they can't do this type of work, there are lots of crimes they can't solve.

What our police need is enough men to do the job, enough mobility to use the men properly, and enough time to solve crimes.

Above all they need our understanding and support. Today they are not getting it.

3 Hindsight and Foresight

It is, of course, axiomatic that our hindsight is better than our foresight, but there certainly shouldn't be such an absolute lack of foresight as we exhibit from time to time.

Looking back to a period when I was much younger than I am now, I remember keenly the arguments of the prohibitionists.

Those were very simple and very deadly.

The prohibitionists pointed out that 90 percent of all crime was caused by alcohol. Therefore, if we abolished liquor, 90 percent of our jails would be unoccupied and those buildings could be used for other purposes. Ninety percent of our law enforcement officers would be liberated for other activities.

I listened to many of the arguments in favor of prohibition. The only argument I ever heard raised against prohibition in those days was that it would cost the state revenue because of the loss of taxes on the sale of liquor. But the prohibitionists pointed out that on a moral issue we should save lives and men and not prostitute our heritage for money.

Of course, everyone knows the answer.

Prohibition was voted in. Prohibition was the legislative king for many years. Courts became absolutely abject in their obedience to the demands of the prohibitionist bloc.

And then, of course, came the horrible aftermath.

Now, the point is that during the time the prohibitionists were making their arguments before various and sundry public gatherings, no one that I know of ever raised his voice to point out what was inevitably going to happen.

No one suggested that it was going to take an ever-increasing army of law-enforcement officers to enforce an unpopular law. No one pointed out that the effect of this law would be to put virtually unlimited money in the hands of the criminal class.

No one advanced the argument that this law would lead to the formation of gangs and the widespread corruption of minor courts and police officers. No one pointed out that this law would lead to hijacking and to murder.

No one prophesied that we would have gangland executions, that we would have widespread rumrunning, that organized crime would get such a start that gangster-dominated organizations would become a part of our country which never could be entirely weeded out.

Why weren't some of these things said?

Simply because people didn't have enough foresight to look ahead and see what was going to happen.

If anybody had raised his voice in a series of such dire predictions he would have been booed and hooted, kicked out of the hall, and thoroughly discredited. The point is that, with all of the millions of people in this country, apparently no one really anticipated what would be the ultimate effect of prohibition.

Now then, we come to the war in Vietnam and its ultimate effect.

We have had lots of shortages in various and sundry fields, but it seems to me that one of the great shortages in the war in Vietnam is that of brains—not at the present time so much as at the time when we took on the responsibilities of trying to turn back the Vietcong.

Is it possible that with the long period of military observation that had gone before we entered this war in earnest, with all of the observers we had on the job, no one had brains enough to look forward and see what was inevitably going to happen?

No one warned the country that we were walking into a veritable quicksand from which there was no reasonable possibility of extricating ourselves and having anything left of national prestige or self-respect.

What were we fighting for?

Where was the enemy?

It is absolutely incredible that we could have engaged in a conflict under such circumstances that a bunch of ill-equipped men, carrying supplies on their backs, were able to wage a war which resulted in bleeding the world's richest country white financially and has meant the sacrifice year after year of many thousands of its best young men.

All for what?

What objectives which can be readily obtained are we fighting for?

I am not talking about glittering generalities or utopian schemes which look well on paper but which are actually beyond the power of practical attainment. I am talking about concrete objectives which we are able to obtain by military pressure of the sort we can bring to bear.

What are they?

Here we are, sending a steady stream of mechanized equipment into a country to fight natives who seem to rely on coolie transportation through jungle areas in order to oppose us, and we are signally inefficient in obtaining any worthwhile objective.

Now, I admit that I don't know exactly what is going on in Vietnam, but I think that in this respect I am like virtually every other American citizen.

Perhaps we are being told now. But I don't think we have been told in the past.

All I know is that we have received assurance from month to month, from year to year, that "the tide of battle has turned"; that the prospect of victory has now been definitely taken from the enemy, in that the fighting is decreasing or is going to stop.

However, all that aside, what I want to discuss is the *effect* of the Vietnam war in this country, rather than the war itself, the effect no one had brains enough to predict.

The psychology of war is peculiar.

To successfully prosecute a war involving the United States we need a white-hot fervor of patriotism.

This patriotism is engendered by directing the mass thinking of our citizens into certain channels. It is the result of bands and of banners, marching men, civilian sacrifices, speeches by orators, editorials and cartoons in the press, inspirational talks from the pulpit, patriotic radio and television programs and a general beating of the drums.

The very nature of the war in Vietnam has been such that we couldn't very well have these things.

In the first place, it isn't a war as this country has known war before; it is simply a series of hostilities in which we are engaged.

At first the press announced that we had twenty thousand troops in Vietnam and we might have to go to thirty thousand.

Apparently at the time that statement was being published we had twice that many troops being rushed to Vietnam, and the buildup continued even after this.

Alarmed parents and disturbed young men whose futures were destined to be affected by the war in Vietnam were given every assurance that we were on the home stretch. Yet year after year we seem to get deeper and deeper in the quicksand.

Moreover the war has always been and will always be an unpopular war. Foreign countries took a good long look at our military activities and disapproved of them.

They quite probably had reason.

We were engaged in a fight where it was not only impossible to deal with hit-and-run tactics successfully, but where we couldn't even identify the enemy. We were killing and maiming civilians without really knowing whether they were friends or enemies, civilians by day or hostile soldiers by night.

There is reason to believe that when a village would get the reputation of sheltering the Vietcong we would send planes with napalm bombs to wipe out the village. Supposedly that would teach other villages a lesson.

Certain it is that in the name of defending organized authority a large number of civilians, including women and young children, were either killed or crippled for life.

From the standpoint of a young man attending college, who can feel the hot breath of the draft board on his neck, it is almost certain that an appraisal of our Vietnam activity would be very critical and hostile indeed.

So it was not surprising that college students began to get restless.

As college youths began to demonstrate, it became apparent that they were demonstrating against the government and against the military, and against organized authority.

They needed to go only a step further to demonstrate against the authority of the university; and soon anything that was unpopular with any particular group could be made the subject of a demonstration.

It wasn't at all necessary to have a majority of the students backing the demonstrators. All that was needed was a handful of articulate individuals making demands in such a manner that a nation sat up in shocked attention.

This made the demonstrators highly newsworthy and their egos were flattered by seeing themselves on nationwide television hookups, making inflammatory speeches.

From there on the situation began to get out of hand.

It is going to continue to be out of hand until we take action to stop it as we eventually and belatedly took steps to stop the evils of prohibition.

The point is that while this situation is developing and continuing to escalate, you and I and every other citizen in the United States are being called on to pay a price which we do not as yet fully realize.

When a situation gets bad enough the police are called in.

The manner in which the police have been used has, in my opinion, been most unwise.

When militant students disrupt classes, police are called to "maintain order on the campus," to "keep the college open."

When the police wade in to make arrests, the bulk of the "students" take to their heels and escape.

After the police get a few truckloads of belligerent militants down to the police station and get them booked, various student organizations start bringing pressure upon the faculty and the administration of the university to get "amnesty."

They don't do this by pleading the justice of the situation; they do this by threatening more, bigger and worse disorders unless their demands are granted.

As a result, in virtually every instance, the authorities throw up their hands, amnesty is granted, the students who have been arrested are released as heroes and the frustrated police have to retire and lick their wounds.

What is all this doing to law enforcement?

Plenty.

As pointed out in the previous chapters, while the police are being held on the campus they are not free to patrol the city.

But even worse for the future, there is a general and growing hostility on the part of the younger generation toward the police. Each time cops are called on campus it reinforces our youth's image of the police as "the enemy."

"Cops" became "fuzz," and "fuzz" became "pigs."

When an Oakland court was trying a Negro on the charge of shooting and killing a police officer, the courthouse steps were picketed by black sympathizers carrying signs saying, "OFF PIGS."

There was a time when making an assault upon an officer of the law was a serious offense, when using profanity in a loud manner in addressing a police officer in public would have resulted in prompt incarceration, when shouting obscenities in public would have caused immediate arrest.

How far have we gone today?

I have in front of me a photograph which gives a graphic illustration of how far we have gone. It is the photograph used on the dust jacket of this book.

This photo shows a police officer running after a young woman who had apparently tried to assault him, then turned and run when he attempted to grab her. The officer has taken after her, and a burly "student," standing slightly to one side, is making a full-arm throw of a stone at the pursuing officer.

This is a photograph which was taken by the International News Service and duly recorded in the daily press.

It has been truly said that a picture is worth ten thousand words.

What is the effect of a picture such as this?

The war in Vietnam, the so-called unrest in the colleges, the vacillating policy of how to deal with the problems and, above all, the business of dragging in the police for confrontations and then letting the police stand as targets for verbal insults, refuse, paper bags, empty bottles and rocks, are having as bad an effect upon our law enforcement as prohibition did.

That effect on law enforcement is going to be with us for many years. It is going to be with us until somebody does something of a positive nature to counteract the damage that is being done. Let us now have some foresight.

4   That Man Is Innocent

I HAVE previously mentioned the fact that good police work takes time and training and freedom from politics. The conscientious officer puts in enough time on a case so he is completely, thoroughly convinced that the man he is arresting, or the man he has arrested, is guilty of the crime charged. The conscientious police officer wants to be very careful not to send an innocent man to prison. But often the officer encounters difficulties due to political influence.

Perhaps one of the best stories to illustrate this point is that of Captain Cross of Detroit.

The story goes back many years, because it is only now that the whole truth can be told.

I played an active part in it and my associate, Dr. Le-Moyne Snyder, also played a part, although at times a somewhat shocked and reluctant role.

My tactics have not always been orthodox, and, while Perry Mason, the fictitious character I created, sometimes skates on very thin ice, there are times when I have been not far behind—when I felt that the end justified the means.

This story of Captain Cross of the Detroit Police Force is inextricably mingled with the story of Louis Gross, a penniless Armenian peddler, who made his living going from door to door, peddling Armenian rugs for what he could get for them, sometimes a good price, sometimes not so good.

A murder was committed within the section of Detroit which is largely peopled by Armenians and persons of Armenian descent.

Some influential people in the community had a corpse on their hands and they needed a fall guy fast.

What better fall guy than Louis Gross, the Armenian rug peddler?

Remember this was quite a few years ago, at a time when police science was not in its present advanced state, at a time when politics, particularly in our large cities, were more corrupt, and at a time when many people, including many judges, felt that it would be impossible under our system of laws to convict an innocent person.

Louis Gross, the rug peddler, without friends, without funds, was arrested, tried and convicted of murder.

Fortunately, Michigan had abolished the death penalty, but Louis Gross was sentenced to prison for life.

Now, Captain W. I. Cross was a thoroughgoing, conscientious police officer who had worked for many years in the Armenian quarter. He had made friends with many influential Armenians who respected him because they found he was fair and honest.

During the period when Louis Gross was being framed, tried and convicted, Captain Cross was serving a term with the Michigan State Police. He returned to the city police in Detroit some two years after the conviction of Louis Gross.

Captain Cross's Armenian friends welcomed him back. They told him all of the news which had happened during his absence. They told him the gossip. They gave him the sort of local information which is priceless to a police officer who has to know what is going on in the community.

Then they began to whisper. There was something wrong with the case of Louis Gross.

Captain Cross was interested. He began an investigation.

Shortly he found himself summoned to appear before one of the city's major politicians.

"I understand you're working on the case of an Armenian named Louis Gross, who was convicted of murder a couple of years ago and is now in prison."

"Yes, I'm making an investigation. I have heard rumors that there was something wrong with that case."

"Lay off of it!"

"How's that?"

"You heard what I said. Lay off it!"

Captain Cross didn't see things quite that way. "Don't you understand?" he said. "I have information that this man may well have been innocent and been convicted as part of a frame-up."

"You heard what I said. Lay off it!"

Captain Cross looked the politician in the eye. "I'm investigating the case," he said.

Within thirty days Captain Cross, very much against his will, was "retired" from the police force, stripped of all authority and no longer drawing a salary.

Captain Cross disappeared.

Louis Gross remained in prison.

Rabbi Joshua Sperka worked as a volunteer chaplain in the Michigan State Prison. Some fifteen years after Louis Gross had been convicted, Rabbi Sperka, in offering spiritual consolation, heard enough of the story of Louis Gross to become convinced that this man may have been innocent.

Rabbi Sperka wrote to me.

Now, one of the things which my associates and myself in the Court of Last Resort wished to avoid at all costs was interesting ourselves in the case of a man who might well have been wrongfully convicted of one particular crime but who was actually a criminal and who should have been convicted for dozens of other crimes.

So I wrote Louis Gross, stating that before we would interest ourselves in his case we would like to know something about his character and background.

I received a letter in which Louis Gross stated, "I have been in one cell block for fifteen years with no complaint."

Quite a character reference.

Since Dr. LeMoyne Snyder at that time was living in East Lansing, Michigan, and this was a Michigan case, I eventually went there and conferred with Dr. Snyder.

We tried to investigate the case of Louis Gross.

At that time a person who had been convicted of murder in Michigan could not appeal the case without a transcript, and he could not furnish a transcript unless he paid for it, and the cost of a transcript was quite high.

We started our investigation and found that in June of 1943 Louis Gross had petitioned the Michigan courts for relief. This was some eleven years after the murder had been committed.

It is to be remembered that when a man has been wrongfully convicted of a crime there is nothing special the authorities need to do to keep him in prison. It is up to the man himself to find some way to get *out* of prison. All the state needs to do to keep him in is to look the other way, so to speak, and that is all there is to it.

The court records of the hearing in 1943 disclosed a strange situation. All the evidence in the Louis Gross case had vanished into thin air. Even if we had put up the money for a transcript, we couldn't have been furnished one because of what had happened.

We let the court records of 1943 speak for themselves:

THE COURT: Now I understand that you have made a thorough search of the records, the stenographer's records, and you find that the stenographic notes of Mr. Harry Kenworthy, who was the official reporter at the examination of Mr. Gross, as well as the official reporter at the time of the taking of the statements in the Gross casse, both in Highland Park and in the prosecutor's office, are also missing.

MR. DE COURSEY: That is right, Your Honor.

THE COURT: And our Mr. Robson was the official court reporter of this court.

MR. DE COURSEY: That is right. The prosecutor's number of the transcribed record of the Gross examination was A-1758. That file is the only one missing from the package containing the examinations of that time, and the book of shorthand notes of Harry Kenworthy, being book No. 196, in which the shorthand notes of the Gross examination were, is also missing from the books in the basement of the County Building.

THE COURT: I have had Mr. Robson's stenographic notes brought to this courtroom and I examined them myself, and all the stenographic notes that he took for that particular year, and some months prior thereto and some months subsequent thereto—all the notes that he took are there except the Gross notes, the Gross murder case notes, and they have been systematically taken out, as there has been a systematic rifling of all records in both this courthouse and the prosecutor's office and also the Justice Court in Highland Park. Not only have the notes disappeared, all statements have disappeared, and even the circuit court file, together with its cover, has disappeared from the county clerk's office.

MR. DE COURSEY: That is the jacket containing the complaint and warrant, and information.

THE COURT: There is nothing before the court in the way of any official records at all, except the motion for new trial filed by Mr. Gross, which leads me to only one conclusion: that whoever did this knew what he was doing, and had access to the files and records in the county clerk's office as well as the basement of the County Building, had access to the records in the prosecuting attorney's office, which should be kept under lock and key, as well as here, and had access to the records, the transcripts and papers in the possession of the Highland Park police department and the Justice Court in Highland Park, and the person or persons who took them certainly knew what they were when they took them. A more systematic theft could not be perpetrated on the people of the state or upon Mr. Gross. I am not naming anybody, but I have my own opinion.

The court went that far but felt it could go no further. Louis Gross was returned to the penitentiary.

Somewhere along the line Dr. LeMoyne Snyder picked up a whisper of the story of Captain Cross and we set about trying to find him.

We learned he had retired to Florida, but no one seemed to know exactly where. However, Dr. Snyder kept on the trail and finally wrote me that he thought he had located Captain Cross.

It seems that the man had grown tired of Florida, had thought about the woods of Northern Michigan and had decided to spend his last years up in the north woods.

So I went to Michigan and Dr. Snyder and I started following clues which eventually led us to a log cabin where we found Captain Cross.

After hearing the story of Captain Cross, we were thoroughly convinced that Louis Gross was innocent and that he had been framed as a fall guy.

But what could we do about it?

Now we come to the part which I have never been able to tell before.

Dr. LeMoyne Snyder and I were leaving New York on a trip to England, Scotland and then to Europe. Dr. Snyder was an old European traveler, but this was my first trip.

Dr. Snyder and I were completely frustrated on that Louis Gross case. I personally didn't like to be brushed under the rug. The matter was preying on my mind.

But what could we do? We were powerless. We had no official status. The authorities had Louis Gross in prison. They intended to keep him there. One honest cop had tried to investigate the case and had come to grief as a result. That showed the sort of thing we were up against.

The reporters who cover the sailings of the transatlantic liners, scanning the passenger list in the hope of a story, caught the names of Dr. Snyder and myself and gave us a routine interview.

Dr. Snyder assured them this trip was in the nature of a vacation.

Then suddenly an idea dawned on me, and without even taking time to think it over, to consider where it might lead, or to consult Dr. Snyder, I started talking.

I told the newspaper reporters that Dr. Snyder was more discreet than I was; that he was not being entirely frank with them, that actually we were going on our trip on a matter of business as well as of pleasure; that we were going to take certain aspects of the case of one Louis Gross of Michigan to some of the outstanding authorities on forensic medicine and crime detection in the British Isles; that we were going to consult some of the prominent criminologists in England and Scotland. This, I pointed out in detail, was the case of Louis Gross who was at present confined in the Michigan Penitentiary, serving a life sentence. No, we couldn't tell the reporters any more than that. In fact, probably I had gone too far in telling them that much.

I knew that the reporters would immediately get in touch with Detroit in order to find out what it was all about.

If you want something kept out of the newspaper, try to get it in. If you want something to appear in the newspaper, try to keep it out, or at least pretend that you're trying to keep it out.

I let the reporters know that I regretted my temporary indiscretion, and they needed only to look at the dour face of Dr. LeMoyne Snyder to see his quite evident disapproval of the whole business.

That was all the newspapers needed.

I felt that this might be an opening wedge in the case. I didn't realize what was to come.

In due course the boat docked at Liverpool. Several English reporters descended on our cabin. They were eager beavers. They had heard that justice in the United States was breaking down and we were appealing to the British experts.

Nothing loath, I told them a few of the facts about the Louis Gross case, and a story written by them was duly cabled across the Atlantic to appear in the Detroit newspapers.

We could get away from the reporters in Liverpool because we were dashing to make connections, but what we hadn't counted on was what happened when we arrived in Glasgow. It is to be remembered that, being carried away by the enthusiasm of the moment, I had said we were submitting evidence to experts in England *and* in Scotland.

We were just back from dinner, looking forward to a restful evening in our room, when a dozen or so determined Scottish reporters came to question us. They had apparently been sent out with instructions to get the detailed story.

There is nothing more determined, nothing more persistent, than a Scottish newspaper reporter and nothing quite as probing as the type of question he can ask.

Dr. Snyder, who had disapproved of the whole caper from the start, sat there with tightly compressed lips and obvious disapproval. I took refuge in talking. I talked and talked.

Whenever I had a chance I gave them the history of the Louis Gross case; whenever they wanted to know specifically what evidence we had brought with us, and what we were expecting to prove by questioning local authorities about a murder which had been committed in the United States some fifteen years earlier, I resorted to a barrage of words.

The impression which I made upon the Scottish newspapermen was somewhat less than favorable.

The impression I made upon my associate, Dr. Le-Moyne Snyder, was distinctly not favorable.

Acting upon impulse, I had decided to wade across what looked like a very safe and narrow stream and suddenly found myself floundering around up to my neck in ice water with a dangerous current running.

But the international wires were flashing back and forth and Detroit was sitting up and taking notice. A long-forgotten case which certain people had considered dead and buried was suddenly assuming international proportions.

The less information newspaper reporters could uncover about the Gross case, the more important it became. *What* did we have which was going to blow the lid off? What were we up to?

The late Gerald K. O'Brien, who was at that time the district attorney in Detroit, was interviewed by reporters and announced that nobody needed to go to England or Scotland to investigate any injustice which had happened within his jurisdiction. By heavens, he'd start his own investigation and he'd get to the bottom of the thing!

This was duly relayed to us by transcontinental telephone and I promptly called the district attorney. We would, I insisted, be only too glad to discontinue our activities in England and Scotland if he was going to make a really good-faith investigation of the case. We would join forces with him. We'd investigate the case together.

He assured me that that was perfectly okay with him.

On our return from Europe, Dr. Snyder and I went to call on Gerald K. O'Brien and found one of the squarest-shooting, most open-minded district attorneys it had ever been our lot to meet.

O'Brien's investigation stirred up things some people didn't want brought to light. Gerald O'Brien and I went to the judge of the District Court, presented the matter to him informally, and the district attorney promised to follow up our discussion with a written motion.

Subsequently Gerald K. O'Brien wrote a letter to the publisher of *Argosy* magazine as follows:

Dear Sir:

I have filed a motion for New Trial, in the Louis Gross case, before the Honorable Thomas F. Maher, of the Wayne County Circuit Court.

As Prosecuting Attorney of Wayne County, I believe it is my duty to protect the innocent as well as prosecute the guilty. This motion will be heard, in all probability, before the next issue of *Argosy* magazine goes to print.

I wish to commend the *Argosy* magazine, Mr. Erle Stanley Gardner, and the whole staff of the magazine for the splendid work they have done in the Gross case.

It is my earnest hope that the Circuit Court will grant the Motion that has been filed.

Sincerely yours,
s/ GERALD K. O'BRIEN
Prosecuting Attorney

The Court granted the motion for a new trial. O'Brien, who was in court, then stood up and moved for a dismissal of the case on the ground that the wrong man had been arrested, tried and convicted.

The case was dismissed and Louis Gross walked out into the sunshine, some seventeen years after he had been convicted, a free man.

Perhaps the ethics of what we did were questionable, but if we hadn't done it Louis Gross would have died in prison for a crime he hadn't committed. Personally, I'd do the same thing all over again under similar circumstances.

I have always believed that in fighting the devil it pays to carry a box of matches.

After his release we heard from Gross with more or less regularity. He married and lived happily for years. Every year at Christmastime we would receive a card from him. His wife, who was a good letter writer, would fill us in on what was happening.

Then about a year ago there was no Christmas card. Later on we had a letter from Mrs. Gross.

Louis Gross had gone out one night to buy a newspaper. He never came back. He was murdered on the street.

Some years ago when I was an Honorary Assistant Attorney General of Texas I was one of the charter members of the Texas Law Enforcement Foundation.

One of the objects of this organization was to see that the police were not hamstrung by politics.

This organization, consisting of a group of some of the most influential citizens in Texas, didn't try to tell the police what to do or what not to do. It was a group of citizens organized to see that the police had a fair deal and that they were kept free from political interference.

There were, of course, many ramifications of such a policy. Among them the organization tried to promote a better understanding of police work on the part of the general public and tried to provide a better climate in which the police could function.

Unless the police have a backlog of citizen support it is very difficult for them to resist the professional politician.

It is in this field that the citizen can be of the greatest assistance.

This does not mean that I advocate any of the so-called citizens' boards of review because, in my opinion, these hamper the efficiency of the police officer.

But the case of Louis Gross shows what can happen when powerful politicians are able to take over and control the police department.

In fact, the story of Louis Gross is completely, absolutely incredible and the full story cannot be told even at this late date because, while I know the facts, I simply can't get the sort of proof which would stand up in court. However, I can state generally that before Gerald K. O'Brien died, he was firmly convinced that the real murderer had appealed to persons with powerful political influence and that Louis Gross had been deliberately selected as a fall guy.

The conscientious police knew or could have known what was happening but were powerless to stand up against the politicians.

Captain Cross tried it and faced complete ruin as a result.

Nothing can be done to rectify the injustice to Captain Cross, but his story illustrates the need for honest citizens to take the police out of politics, and to keep them out, to stand back of the honest cops, to have some sort of a forum or committee to which the honest cop can appeal when he is being blocked by or kicked around by the politicians.

Police and politics shouldn't mix.

5 Keep the Good Guys

Good policemen are more interested in seeing that justice is done than in making arrests. And a thoroughly competent police officer has his own built-in lie detector, an uncanny ability to sense something wrong about a case.

Time after time I have ridden with police officers who have demonstrated this ability to separate the sheep from the goats, to pick up the right man at the right time at the right place for questioning and to let the honest man go on his way.

The officers insist that they just "have a feeling," but all good police seem to know that one of the necessary requirements is to be alert at all times.

Take the case of C.W.S., for instance.

This man had twice been convicted of burglaries, and when three motels were robbed near where he was living, police picked him up for questioning because of his record and the fact that he answered the description of the man who had committed the robberies.

Three of the victims at the motels positively identified him as the robber. C.W.S. was convicted and sent to Chino Prison in California for from five years to life.

Then a Los Angeles Police sergeant, Hank Seret, who was processing a robbery suspect on November 25th,

1963, became suspicious, subjected his prisoner to a searching inquiry and found that this man was the perpetrator of the motel robberies.

Manley J. Bowler, Chief Deputy District Attorney, promptly presented a motion for the release of C.W.S. The motion was granted by the courts and C.W.S. walked out of prison a free man.

Or let us take the case of R.M.W., arrested for holding up service stations in Bell and in Inglewood, California.

R.M.W., who had been released from prison after a three-year sentence for grand theft, was arrested on a warrant charging him with the robberies. He was "positively identified" from photographs and later was picked out of police lineups by the victims.

Lt. George R. Wagner, a Bell detective, wasn't entirely satisfied. There were circumstances in the case which, to his eye as a trained police officer, had led him to believe there had been a mistake.

Lieutenant Wagner went to work and, after a painstaking investigation, was able to unearth facts which convinced District Attorney Evelle J. Younger, of Los Angeles, that the wrong man had been arrested and identified.

District Attorney Younger wrote a letter to Chief R. H. Parks, of Bell, commending the work of Lieutenant Wagner.

District Attorney Younger said in part in his letter, "The particular efforts of Lt. Wagner merit public attention, not alone because of his dedication and integrity, but also because the public too often fails to learn of the hundreds of similar cases in which, through the efforts of police officers, the innocent are protected."

For many people who think of cops only in terms of arrests this puts the police in a new light. To persons who regularly follow television programs it also puts district attorneys in a new light.

These are stories of the cops who are "good guys" and of the district attorneys who are "good guys."

It is, of course, unfortunately true that there are men in both categories who are "bad guys." However, those people have already had plenty of publicity and these illustrations are for the purpose of reminding us that there are "good guys" too.

But good, expert law-enforcement officers don't grow on trees.

It is generally conceded that it takes from three to five years to turn a rookie into a really first-class cop, no matter how much aptitude he may have. He gets his training in a variety of ways.

A number of universities throughout the country have courses in police science and issue degrees. One of the first of these courses was instituted by my friend and colleague, Dr. LeMoyne Snyder, at Michigan State University.

The FBI has a training school for prospective agents which is tops in the field. Here men are taught how to investigate, how to prepare cases, how to handle firearms, how to make arrests, how to preserve and interpret evidence.

Most of the large cities have police academies.

A relatively young man, alert and intelligent, with muscular build and good coordination, makes an application for police work. If he passes his preliminary examinations he is sent to the city's police academy where he is instructed in the practical side of police work, taught to evaluate evidence, to handle firearms and to shoot with accuracy.

The late Captain Frances G. Lee sponsored seminars

in homicide investigation at the Harvard Medical School in Boston.

I was privileged to attend two of these seminars.

Captain Lee was a remarkable character; a woman no longer young, independently wealthy, she had made a hobby of legal medicine, police science and homicide investigation. She had been appointed an honorary member of the New Hampshire State Police, with the rank of captain.

Her seminars at the Harvard Medical School were not for rookies, but were for state police officers from the various states, most of whom were selected by the governors of their respective states as being outstanding officers. The class was strictly limited in number and there were lectures on various aspects of homicide investigation and police science.

There are many phases of police science, however, which can no more be learned by listening to lectures or reading books than one can learn how to become a pugilist by taking a correspondence course in boxing.

Captain Lee had spent a fortune on a series of miniature models of various crimes which had actually been investigated during the course of years by the New England medical examiners.

These models were in glass cases and were on the scale of one inch to the foot, their details worked out with care.

If, for instance, a miniature figure of an officer were shown in uniform writing in a notebook, one could be certain that the pencil, which was hardly bigger in diameter than a match, was an actual pencil with lead in it, and that the notes in the notebook had actually been made with that pencil. In fact, many of the details had been worked out under a microscope by highly trained artisans.

She had approximately two dozen of these miniature

models and each member of the class would be assigned problems related to two of them.

The problems came from real life and represented actual cases. All of the clues were there. If the student was bright enough to solve the assigned cases, he could well be proud of his accomplishment.

Some cities have simulated actual problems as a part of their police training program.

When I was in one of our large cities the chief of police took me into two rooms in the police academy. Synthetic crimes had been committed in these rooms. Wax figures in life size represented the corpses as the police officer would find them on being called in for an investigation. The various clues which an officer should note and appraise were, of course, lying around on the floor, on the table, in the ashtrays, etc.

It was up to the rookie as an investigating officer to enter the room, appraise the scene, take his notebook and jot down all significant details, take measurements when necessary, draw diagrams, and then develop a theory as to what had happened.

It will probably come as a shock to the readers of many detective stories, but the trained investigator can usually tell if a body has been moved after life has been extinct for any reasonable period of time.

I remember one case which I was privileged to work on with Dr. LeMoyne Snyder where he was able to work out a sequence of events from a photograph.

The nearly naked body of a young woman had been found in a stream bed beneath a wooden bridge. Photographs had, of course, been taken.

Dr. Snyder and I were called in by a big metropolitan newspaper to assist the authorities in solving the puzzling case.

We asked to look at the photographs.

The district attorney hesitated for a moment, then said, "I don't know whether the fault is with the negative or the print, but the photograph of the body shows a peculiar circle on one hip which was not there when the body was discovered—at least, several trained investigators studied the body carefully and all are agreed that there was no circle there at that time."

The answer was that the circle had actually been there but the coloration was such that it showed only on the photographic emulsion of the film. The naked eye couldn't see it. It turned out to be one of the key clues in the solution of the case.

The work of a police officer is dangerous and demanding. Not everyone is suited to be a policeman by temperament or otherwise. Not everyone can take the training and develop into a first-class officer.

We need desperately to keep the ones that are first-class.

What with increasing taxes and increasing expenses on the part of all municipalities, it is often difficult to ask the citizens to furnish sufficient pay increases to keep the good men on in the department. But unless the public wakes up and takes definite steps to see that we do our share by paying our police properly we'll be in trouble.

In a jurisdiction which I investigated at one time, there was a turnover of something like 80 percent of the law enforcement officials within a five-year period.

In other words, by the time the rookie got enough training to enable him to become a first-class police officer, he had developed enough talents so that he was in demand in other labor markets. Usually through marriage and the desire to raise a family, the man's living expenses had increased to a point where he couldn't turn down the more lucrative offer of some other branch of work.

Just what does this mean? It means that those veterans

who remained on the force had to put in the bulk of their time, not in catching criminals or working to prevent crime, but in training new rookies who, in turn, would for the most part get their training and then drift off to better paying jobs.

If a city manager bought twenty acres of orchard, planted it with trees that would come into bearing only at the end of three years, and then every third year would cut down 80 percent of the trees in order to plant fresh ones, he wouldn't hold his job as manager very long.

Yet that is essentially what was happening in this jurisdiction which wasn't taking care to protect its investment in the training of law enforcement officers.

But there are considerations other than folding money —for instance, public esteem and things that satisfy human dignity.

That is why I am so concerned about the present situation, where highly trained, competent men are called upon to stand in line against a bunch of hippies or immature college kids and be the target for everything from spit to rocks.

How long will our good policemen stay around to take this sort of thing? There are easier ways of making a living and lots of other ways to make more money.

Please remember that good policemen are not only our best protection against criminals, they are our best protection against the innocent being wrongfully accused, arrested and convicted. So let's keep the good guys, and to do so we must pay them not only with money but with respect.

6 Citizen Brutality

WHILE it is poor business to use police in a static confrontation with students or other dissidents, it is necessary to call upon the police when the situation escalates into lawlessness.

When there is a riot there is urgent need for law-enforcement officers.

A riot is a sinister activity, and while it may be spontaneously engendered, some riots are carefully planned.

In California, cities not only have their own police force, but since they are a part of the county the police can be reinforced by a sheriff and numbers of deputies. As an ace in the hole the authorities can also rely on the state militia—and in times of emergency members of the highway patrol can be called in.

On the other hand, this very system makes for a complication in that the police force is under the authority of the chief of police. The chief of police, in turn, is either directly or indirectly under the authority of the mayor, while the sheriff, as an elected officer, is responsible only to the voters. And the governor, as the chief executive of the state, is responsible only to his own conscience, at least until the next election.

It would seem that these various law-enforcement authorities should have some liaison, some definite understanding *in advance* of riots so that they will know just what they are going to do and just how it is to be done and, above all, *when* it is to be done.

Riots may start spontaneously. For example, a policeman seeks to arrest a young man of a minority race for driving a stolen car. A group of angry protestors gathers and starts giving the officer a bad time. The officer radios for help. The ranks of the protestors become augmented. Someone starts throwing rocks at the police who are arriving to help. Suddenly this situation erupts into a riot.

On the other hand, some riots are deliberately planned and have all the aspects of a limited civil war.

Anyone would be naïve indeed not to realize that there are within our country forces which are seeking to overthrow our government and to undermine *all* authority.

There are also militant groups among the minorities that seek to instill hatred for the government and all governmental institutions.

Some of these people are very clever. They have reduced to a science the art of cultivating discontent, of formulating "issues" and recruiting enthusiastic young people to go to all sorts of lengths in promoting the "brave new world."

It seems incredible that people with average human intelligence could be prevailed upon to act on the assumption that by tearing down everything we have, something new and better will be found in the ruins.

If I were living in a house that was smaller than I wanted and needed a lot of modernization, I would call in a good architect and we would carefully start remodeling. I wouldn't come in with a hammer and crowbar, rip the doors off their hinges, smash all the windows, pile the furniture in the middle of the room and then set fire to it, with the idea that by some magic a new house more suited to my needs would spring up out of the ashes.

Yet we have misguided but enthusiastic college youths who are undoubtedly sincere in their belief that the first thing to do is to tear down the whole existing order and trample it into anarchy in order to "cure the evils" of the present social system.

These people don't realize the extent to which they are being victimized, how deliberately it is being done, how skillfully it is handled, or the sinister nature of the forces which are behind the thinking that brings these tactics into existence.

I had a friend who was talking with a police officer at one of the college confrontations where the situation was rapidly deteriorating.

The officer pointed out one individual and said, "Keep your eye on that man. He is moving from person to person, from group to group, urging them to stand up for their 'rights,' exhorting the people to violence."

The officer then named several colleges at which this same person had been seen at the time of the confrontations doing the same thing.

"But," the officer predicted, "just as soon as violence starts, that man will be long gone. You can't find him. *He* won't participate in any violence. At that time he won't even be a part of the crowd. He's got his getaway already arranged. It doesn't fit in with his plans to be arrested."

No one knows exactly how many of these really intelligent revolutionists are at work among the susceptible and among the enthusiastic members of the younger generation, but there are many of them—too many.

Then we have riots like the one which occurred over the issue of the so-called People's Park in Berkeley.

If the atmosphere hadn't first been conditioned by confrontations, riots and a general undermining of authority, it is hardly conceivable that such an issue as the People's Park could have triggered a riot.

The University of California owned some property near the University on which it intended to build at the proper time. In the meantime, the place began to be peopled by a heterogeneous assortment of individuals.

Children used it as a playground, and the so-called "street people" began to move in.

The street people and the hippies are peculiar developments of a philosophy which was advocated a generation or so ago in which the word "discipline" was anathema. Children were never disciplined. They were permitted to do whatever they wanted, the idea being that any restriction cramped their little characters; they grew up doing as they pleased and they never had to do anything they didn't want to do.

In this world of theirs w-o-r-k became a dirty four-letter word—about the only four-letter word that was really dirty.

How these people get by is something of a mystery. Apparently many of them are still catered to by indulgent parents. They live in a world which is a community of its own. They have thrown morals out of the window; cleanliness is a forgotten virtue. They live packed in rooms like sardines. Some of them live by petty crimes. Some of them live in a sort of communal arrangement and others are supported by parents who are usually far removed from the scene.

Various people began to use this block of vacant property owned by the University of California. Evidently some children played there. People installed some swings, and the hippies and street people made use of the property.

It is difficult to learn all the details. There were no

toilet facilities on the property, yet some of the street people seemed to live there, more or less camping out.

The University decided to put a fence around the property, which then was called the "People's Park" by those who wanted to keep on using it.

Agitators promptly proceeded to seize upon the construction of this fence as an "issue."

The People's Park was being taken away from the people. "Down with the fence! Start a march of protest! Go take the park by force!"

It seems incredible that an occasion such as this could have caused all of this trouble or that it could have led to a riot, but it did.

This time the confrontation had vicious tones. It wasn't necessary for the agitators to escalate a conflict. It had all been too carefully planned for that.

Protestors marched along the street; the police tried to control them and the protestors became an angry mob. Police cars were smashed. Rocks, bottles and other projectiles were hurled at the police. People had gathered not only along the streets but on the rooftops bordering the streets.

On the rooftops—now, that's interesting.

How did the people get to the rooftops? What was the idea in gathering there? Who were these people?

And once on the rooftops, the people started hurling rocks, bottles, cement blocks and pieces of construction steel. This construction steel consisted of rods of varying lengths used to reinforce concrete. The rods had been conveniently cut into lengths which were suitable for throwing. They were, of course, very deadly missiles.

One of these missiles struck a police car and went entirely through the steel body of the car. Some of them struck police and inflicted serious injuries. This was, in short, a full-fledged riot.

But how did all of these missiles get up on the roofs of the buildings? That's a peculiar place to look for deadly missiles.

I am acquainted with a newspaper reporter who tells me that he has evidence that all of this ammunition was surreptitiously carried up to the roofs of the buildings *the day before the riot.*

I have personally talked with a party who has a place of business on the street where the rioting took place. He says the "ammunition" of rocks, cement blocks and steel rods was brought in by truck the day before the riot and transported to the roofs in sacks.

The authorities retaliated first with tear gas, then with shotguns loaded with bird shot and then with shotguns loaded with buckshot.

Several rioters were wounded and one individual was killed.

Immediately a great hue and cry went up from the rioters' sympathizers. The man who was killed was a "bystander"—a spectator who had climbed to the roof of a building so he could the better watch what went on below.

In any event, the situation had blossomed into a riot and the man, bystander or not, was part of a mob of people on a roof. Some of these people were engaged in throwing deadly missiles.

Once a planned riot gets under way there isn't any question but what an "innocent bystander" has put himself in danger.

A man who goes to a place where there is a hostile confrontation with police, who climbs to the roof of a building and finds there piles of rocks, bottles and spears of building steel which people are hurling at the police, and then elects to stay there can well be called a "bystander," but hardly an "innocent bystander."

Sheriff Madigan, of Alameda County, spoke his piece. He said, in effect, that his men were confronted by a hostile mob which was moving in; that his deputies would have been overwhelmed if they hadn't resorted to shotguns; that under similar circumstances they would do the same thing again.

That statement and the buckshot had a salubrious effect.

A later group, consisting of an estimated thirty thousand people, marched in the so-called People's Park Protest. By that time the state militia had been called and the march was peaceful and orderly.

In the riot several policemen had been seriously injured, police cars had been smashed up—all for what?

It is indicative of the extent to which these highly intelligent agitators have been sowing the seed of discord that such a situation could have erupted over a "People's Park."

The University owned the property. It had been purchased for a price of more than a million dollars. Residents in the neighborhood complained to the University that the property and adjoining properties had been used not only as a dumping ground for garbage but as impromptu toilets.

To think that the decision to fence this private property could have been used as an "issue" to trigger a carefully planned riot is indicative of the tensions under which we live.

It is also significant that one college professor went on the air and stated that the people were entitled to the park because the people were the real owners of everything.

This nation became great because it believed in a philosophy of work. People went to college to acquire an education so they could later engage in a constructive program which would bring wealth into existence, wealth which contributed to the power and welfare of this country.

Now we have a group of red-eyed revolutionists who are circulating throughout our colleges, advocating a theory of tearing down existing institutions, not to substitute something better, but simply to get rid of the faults in our existing scheme of things.

According to this philosophy, if mice are in your house doing damage, you simply set fire to the house, stand on the outside, watch it burn and then trust to luck that somehow you are going to find a roof over your head that night.

I am old-fashioned. I am a "square." I believe that when a person gets old enough to work he should put his shoulder to the wheel and contribute something to the economic stability of the country. I believe that he should develop his own talents and his own character by good, hard, honest work.

I am also sufficiently modern to realize that there are many evils in our civilization which need fixing. We need the young and enthusiastic outlook of the college student to help us acquire the proper perspective.

But that is a far cry from tearing everything down in the hope that complete chaos will somehow be better than what we have.

There comes a biological time in the late teens and early twenties when the intellectual fledglings become conscious of their expanding mental powers and badly overestimate their capabilities. They look patronizingly at the old fogies and want to throw them out. This is a normal development of intellectual adolescence.

But this new creed of long-haired idleness, of drifting aimlessly with no goal in sight, is something far removed from the normal growth.

Let the hippies and the street people take over and we will not only cease to be a first-class nation, we will be no nation at all.

Somewhere along the line common sense should rear its head before it is shouted down by the tumult of the hippies and the street people. Indulgent parents who send their mature offspring money for doing nothing and the damn fools in general who don't know what it's all about or what is really going on had better wake up.

The pathetic part of all this is that so many of these dissident students do have a legitimate grievance. Militant agitators capitalize on these grievances and on the enthusiasms of these youthful zealots to get them to seek the wrong remedies.

All of which is one more reason why we need a strong, fully professional, updated police force, and improved channels of communication with the young men and women in our colleges so that they, too, have a better understanding of police work.

Recently some of the student agitators have promulgated the doctrine that because the police are armed with guns it is only "self-defense" for the students to arm themselves with bottles, rocks and various other projectiles.

Beating the police to the punch and hurling these items at the officers constitutes "self-defense"? We need "defense" against our duly constituted law officers?

Words can be twisted and distorted into all sorts of meanings and this is the new meaning of "self-defense."

And it is the same distorted use of words which enables the agitators to talk about "police brutality."

When an agitator throws a bottle at the police he is "an innocent bystander" resorting to "self-defense." But if the officer charges in with an upraised club that becomes a shocking example of "police brutality."

Police are only human. After they have stood so much abuse and are then called on to move in to make arrests, human nature being what it is, many of the police are going to hit the line of dissidents a little harder than might otherwise be the case.

But where has there been a case of police brutality which wasn't first triggered by someone resorting to the type of "citizen brutality" that started the whole sequence of events?

7   Armed and Dangerous

JACK HARGRAVE, a veteran officer and police detective, has now retired from the Denver Police Force.

During the time when he was an officer on active duty Hargrave and I spent quite a bit of time together and we still carry on quite a correspondence.

Hargrave, who despite retirement maintains an active interest in police work, keeps me posted on new wrinkles in the field of police science and of law enforcement and in the field of criminal activities. Before his retirement, whenever I was in Denver, we spent a great deal of time together in patrol cars.

Hargrave is a warm, personal friend, and quite frequently I was a dinner guest at his house before going out with him on night patrol duty. I was always impressed by the manner in which he would get up from the table, say good-by to his family and then start out on his round of nightly duties. No one ever said anything, but there was always the feeling that there was more than a remote possibility that one of these nights Jack might not come back.

One night I had been on patrol with him and he had dropped me at my hotel shortly after midnight. A few nights after that, at a time when I, fortunately—or unfortunately—was not with him, Jack's radio car received what seemed like a routine call to go to an apartment house to investigate a disturbance on the seventh floor.

It happened that Hargrave was alone that night, although generally he had a partner on his patrols. The weather was cold and raw.

Hargrave entered the lobby of the apartment house, intent upon going to the seventh floor to investigate the disturbance. His coat was buttoned up and he walked casually across the lobby to the elevator, his mind occupied with the mechanics of reaching the seventh floor.

Suddenly from the direction of the stairs a figure materialized and started walking toward him.

Hargrave has that sixth sense which veteran officers develop. It is a sort of radar which functions at a time of danger. Jack doesn't know how it works. He only knows that he has it, and I have seen it work.

Hargrave immediately sensed that the man who was walking across the lobby toward the exit was the man who had been causing the disturbance on the seventh floor. He also knew that the man was armed and dangerous.

With great presence of mind Hargrave realized that he had been caught at a disadvantage, that he wouldn't be able to get at his gun in time to do any good and that the only thing to do was to ignore the other man and walk casually along toward the elevator until he was past the man he wanted; then he could whirl and have the advantage of approaching his quarry from behind.

It wasn't intended to be that way.

The man waited until he was just a step or two from Hargrave, then he jerked his hand out from his coat, pointing a vicious automatic at Jack's belly, cursing all cops and saying that no blankety-blankety-blank cop was going to take him alive.

With that he pulled the trigger.

There was a faint click.

Hargrave grappled with the man. Together they wrestled across the floor of the lobby. Eventually Hargrave subdued him, took his gun away, got handcuffs on his wrists and marched him off to jail.

Hargrave's fellow officers regarded the gun with wonder. It was an automatic, fully loaded, and apparently in perfect working order. It turned out, however, that the man had been carrying it in a pocket with some matches and a small splinter from one of the matches had worked down into the firing mechanism so that the hammer didn't quite strike the firing pin with sufficient force to explode the shell.

After they had the gun in the police laboratory they tried to fire it and it worked perfectly, shooting and ejecting in rapid succession, sending forth a fusillade of potential death.

This story is illustrative of the work a cop has to face every day—sudden danger at a time when the officer may least expect it.

Suppose you are an officer patrolling in a car and someone driving a car at a rather high rate of speed shoots on past you.

The driver is a young kid of seventeen or eighteen, and something in the manner in which he drives the car arouses your suspicions.

You swing in behind the car, pick up the license number, put it on the police radio and ask for a report.

Seconds later a report comes in that confirms your suspicion. The car is a stolen automobile.

The driver is just a young, slim-waisted kid, probably out for a joy ride, but you turn on the red light, edge in behind him and give the button of the siren a touch.

The kid pulls off to the side of the road and looks

back with an expression on his face which says quite plainly, "Who, me?"

You get out of your car and start toward him.

Are you dealing with a frightened kid who has stolen a car with the idea of taking a joy ride, or are you dealing with one of these crazy young punks, perhaps hopped up on drugs, who is sitting there with a gun in his lap? When you take a couple more steps will he suddenly pull up the gun and try to shoot his way out?

If you take the precautions you really should take and pull your own gun as you approach the car, then tell the kid to get his hands up and keep them in sight, you are in for trouble.

The young boy's mother will tell of police brutality, about how her son, who had borrowed a car from a friend without knowing that it was stolen, was stopped by the police who covered her dear son with a Magnum revolver and threatened to blow him apart unless he put up his hands, kept them in plain sight and got out of the car.

She will write letters to the press, claiming that such tactics shouldn't be used on an innocent boy who had merely borrowed a car from a friend whom he had met at a party and whose name he can't recall at the moment.

Suppose there are two people in the car. Suppose that you stop them out on a lonely stretch of road and approach the car to ask for a driver's license and information as to what the occupants are doing.

Throughout the United States many of your brother officers who have done just that are now lying six feet beneath the sod, their names enscrolled on memorial tablets.

There is hardly a moment when you are on duty when you are not in danger. You have to be self-reliant, alert and yet tactful. It is a tough combination.

If you take the precautions which are really necessary

to insure your own safety, you are going to face a storm of public protest. Police brutality! Officers brandishing guns! Innocent citizens who have done nothing more than go through a boulevard stop terrorized by callous police, forced at gunpoint to show their identification.

If you act on the assumption that you are dealing with the average citizen, the time is going to come when, as you approach the automobile ahead, you will suddenly see the black muzzle of a gun protrude from the open car window.

Then you will see a flash. You may, or may not, ever hear the roar of the explosion which follows.

People who read about it will shrug their shoulders and say, "Well, after all, the guy was a cop. He had a gun. Why did he walk up on a car, leaving himself wide open that way?"

8 The Death Penalty

ONE OF the problems in the area of crime is punishment. The most severe punishment is the death penalty.

I am opposed to the death penalty because I think it is of questionable value as a deterrent to crime, and because standards for imposing and enforcing it vary so widely from court to court and case to case.

I am particularly against the death penalty because it is so utterly irrevocable, and I have known so many cases of innocent men who have been wrongfully convicted of murder.

I am also opposed to it because it is such a lottery. Men who commit cold-blooded, deliberate murders are often able to defeat the death penalty, while others who are guilty of murders under circumstances which could possibly bring the death penalty are simply clobbered by stern-faced jurors who want to enforce the letter of the law.

Opponents of the death penalty claim that no man who has money behind him has ever been legally executed; that the death penalty is for the poor and the unfortunate. There is a lot of truth in that claim.

I am opposed to the death penalty except in one type

of case, and that is where officers of the law are killed while in the performance of their duties.

Let me give you some cases out of my own personal experience which show you why I have come to these conclusions.

There is a goodly amount of smuggling from Mexico into the United States. One illegal commodity which is now in demand in the United States is agricultural labor known in the vernacular as "wetbacks," because the prototype of this group had wet backs from swimming the Rio Grande from Mexico into the United States. Wetbacks are impoverished Mexicans who have to work in order to eat. Although the wages these people receive in Mexico are often abysmally low by American standards, the Mexican has to find a way to live and he wants work and he wants better wages. Under these circumstances, it is not surprising that there is considerable traffic in human smuggling.

In addition to this human traffic there is the traffic in marijuana, which is particularly lucrative and particularly vicious.

One of the lessons taught us by prohibition—or a lesson which *should* have been taught us by prohibition—is that whenever there is a large public demand for anything it is exceedingly difficult, if not impossible, to pass punitive laws which will keep that demand from being supplied.

The more stringent the laws, the higher the price of supply.

That is turning out to be true in respect to marijuana. Hundreds of tons are smuggled into the United States in a never-ending stream.

However, let's take a look at the smug complacency of the do-it-by-law faction.

Many rural newspapers, and a few in the larger cities,

often publish news items of twenty, thirty, or fifty years ago.

The newspaper in Chico, in northern California, under date of 1957 published a quotation from its issue of thirty years earlier regarding the drug traffic.

Here is what the item said:

"The narcotics problem is very largely solved," said W. Bruce Phillips of San Francisco, secretary of the Alameda County Pharmaceutical Association, today in an address to the members of the Rotary Club at the Hotel Oaks.

The lecturer indicated that federal and state laws governing the importation and distribution of narcotics in the United States were so stringent that there has been a great deal less use of narcotics than the public has been led to believe through the distribution of literature by propagandists.

Many years ago, when the Sunday newspaper magazine, *This Week,* was just starting, I wrote a serial for it dealing with a smuggling plot and mentioned marijuana. Back came the story with a note from the editors asking that I change the copy. It seemed that the FBI had written all editors asking them never to mention marijuana in their columns.

The FBI didn't want the American people ever to find out about marijuana.

Today the main contraband traffic consists in growing marijuana in Mexico, drying it and compressing it into bricks, smuggling it into the United States and selling it.

Mexico is on the metric system as far as weights are concerned and the weight of marijuana is estimated in kilos. A kilo is two and two-tenths pounds. It may sell for as little as ten dollars a kilo in Mexico; in California a wholesale shipment of marijuana is worth fifty dollars a kilo. The wholesaler splits the kilo up into smaller packages and it is delivered to pushers at a price which nets the pusher a hundred dollars a kilo on up.

The retail rate of sale after the marijuana is made into cigarettes, of course, represents a terrific profit. These cigarettes *may* sell for from fifty cents to a dollar apiece.

Therefore, the marijuana traffic is immensely profitable and, as a result, quite widespread. Just how widespread no one knows.

Temecula, in southern California, where I have my main headquarters, is located in a strategic position as far as drug traffic is concerned. Highway 395, which stretches north from San Diego, is joined near Temecula by the highway which comes from the Imperial Valley through Warner Springs. A favorite place for the Border Patrol, which is looking for wetbacks, is to locate a checkpoint just north of Temecula, or at another point just south of Temecula.

Temecula enjoys some of the best climate in southern California. For the most part, it escapes the searing heat of the desert, and within a few miles of Temecula there are avocado, orange and lemon groves. More recently retirement communities have opened up; many real estate subdivisions have come into existence, and there are numerous golf courses dotting the country between Temecula and the outskirts of San Diego to the south.

June 16, 1967, was a warm, sunny day and the sunset was followed by velvety darkness.

Two young Border Patrolmen were ordered to go from the Temecula checkpoint to establish another checkpoint on the road from Warner Springs at a historic place known as Oak Grove, where there was an old Butterfield Stage Station and, more recently, campsites and a trailer park.

Oak Grove is midway in the mountains between the desert of the Imperial Valley and the Temecula Valley. There is a huge live oak growing over a wide place in the road, and it was beneath this tree that the Border Patrol-men parked their cars.

On this night the two Border Patrolmen, Theodore Newton, Jr., age twenty-four, and George Azrak, age twenty-one, set up a checking point. They had a jeep and also one of the official Border Patrol cars.

They went about the mechanics of putting up the road-block, setting out signs, which would be illuminated by the headlights of approaching automobiles, ordering traffic to stop and bearing the statement that federal officers were on the job.

Theodore Newton had a wife and two children. He was a graduate of the Border Patrol Training Academy but had had less than one year's active duty.

George Azrak was a recruit and not as yet a graduate of the Academy.

Quite obviously, these men were young and inexperienced insofar as coping with hardened, desperate criminals was concerned, although they understood their duties and were quite capable of handling the routine assignment of checking traffic for "wetbacks."

At 2:40 A.M. on June 17, these two Border Patrolmen reported by radio. Everything was going okay on a routine assignment.

A few hours later, when they were scheduled to go off duty, they didn't show up to report. Still later, when they failed to answer their radio, a checkup was made and it was found that both men and cars had vanished from the checkpoint.

Still later, when a search was instituted, their jeep was found parked under a tree some distance from the place where the roadblock had been established but still within sight of the highway. There was no sign of the Border Patrol car.

Thoroughly alarmed, the department called in the

services of an airplane and later of a helicopter, all without results.

Then a man at the small town of Anza, some miles to the north, stated that he had seen a Border Patrol car drive by shortly after daylight that morning.

Between Oak Grove and Anza there are miles and miles of rugged mountains covered with mesquite, oak, chaparral, redshank, manzanita, sagebrush, mountain lilac or buckthorn.

From these mountains long, dry barrancas stretch down in a whole series of drainage fingers to the lower country. In places there are roads up these barrancas or canyons which can be traversed by four-wheel-drive cars and, in some places where the hillsides have lent themselves to clearings and cultivations, there are hayfields with service roads running up to them from an isolated ranch house which may be quite some distance away.

For the most part the country is wild, barren and deserted.

Since the FBI has jurisdiction over the investigation of crimes against federal officers, it established a law-enforcement command post in the Forestry Station at Oak Grove. Volunteer groups offered their services, were briefed, then were assigned certain areas to search out systematically.

Following the report by the witness at Anza, the search began to converge along this wild, rugged country, first, because the patrol car had been seen by the witness at Anza; second, because this part of the country was about the only place where the car *could* have been concealed, where it couldn't have been found as a result of the intensive air and ground search that had been called into operation.

The search was futile. The air search disclosed nothing; even the helicopter found no trace of the car.

Enter the Four-Wheel-Drive Buffs.

Throughout this section of southern California there are various four-wheel-drive aficionados. They have clubs and, from time to time, have "meets" where they get together, make a central camp and from this camp run tours of a type designed to test the skill and daring of the driver, laying out courses through deep sand, up steep hills, along ridges, down rocky slopes and through various natural hazards.

When word spread that two Border Patrolmen were missing, had probably been abducted and perhaps murdered, the four-wheel-drive club talked with officers at the command post and were invited to assist in the organized search.

One group of drivers was assigned to take charge of the search on the right-hand side of the road. Another group was to take charge of searching the left-hand side. One of the drivers assigned to the job of following any leads on the right-hand side of the main road followed a fair road up to a ranch house and then fought his way for several miles up along the barranca, following an old, old road and signs of recent wheel tracks.

After several miles he came to the head of the canyon, where there was a little ramshackle cabin, long deserted, and a clump of trees furnishing shade and concealment.

The driver saw that a car had been driven far under the overhanging branches of the trees and that additional branches had been cut and placed on the car until it was completely covered and could not be seen from the air. He recognized it as the missing patrol car.

Somewhat fearful for his own safety, he used his Citizen's Band radio to put out an SOS.

Shortly reinforcements arrived.

There could be no doubt about it. This was the missing car. A posse of grim-faced men entered the cabin.

What they saw was enough to cause even these veterans to recoil with horror.

This old, unpainted one-room shack had, at one time, contained a bunk, a table, an iron stove and a bench.

In front of the stove, their arms thrust through and under the stove legs, the wrists of each handcuffed to the wrists of the other, was all that was left of the two Border Patrolmen.

It was a grim spectacle.

They had been forced to sit down, their arms entwined under the stove, their wrists handcuffed; and they then had been executed in cold blood, apparently shot with their own guns, shot through the back of the head.

One of the men had been shot twice, once through the chest from the back, then through the head from the back.

It was so shocking the men who saw it were hard put to fight back nausea. The heat, the blood, the spattered brains, and the lazy, droning flies gathering about the bodies made the spectacle unforgettable.

If it hadn't been for the assistance of the four-wheel-drive fans, weeks or months might have elapsed before the bodies had been found.

Sam Hicks, who is my ranch foreman, and I took one of my four-wheel-drive cars and went up the canyon to the shack. This was some time after the bodies had been removed. It was a long drive and only someone who knew the country would have known anything about this road or the location of the shack.

Once the cabin had been found, however, the very isolation of the place furnished its own clue.

The FBI, which poured a whole army of agents into the case, rightfully concluded that the abductors, whoever they might have been, wouldn't have taken these two young Border Patrolmen on the long trip up that barranca unless they had known something of the country; and, in order to have known something about the country and particularly that this old deserted cabin was situated way up that canyon, far from any other place of human occupancy, some of the abductors must have lived, worked, or hunted in the vicinity.

The FBI also deduced that the only persons who could have committed a crime of this sort were hardened, professional criminals.

Therefore, they were faced with a question—what hardened, professional criminals would have reason to abduct the Border Patrolmen rather than submit to a search? The answer, of course, was professional dope smugglers with a shipment of dope that was too valuable to risk losing.

Such men were likely to have records.

So the FBI started searching records to find men who were, or had been, engaged in dope smuggling, who had lived in this part of the country under such circumstances that they might be expected to know of this long-abandoned cabin.

Soon four names were uncovered: Victor J. Bono, twenty-eight years old, tall, catfooted, who had previously been arrested with something over two thousand pounds of marijuana, and who had jumped his bail; Florencio Mationg, short, barrel-chested, who had already served an eleven-year sentence; Harold Montoya, with a record of arrests for battery, burglary, robbery and statutory rape; and Alfred Montoya, a brother of Harold, with a record of housebreaking, car tampering, grand theft auto, receiving stolen property, armed robbery and escape from prison.

Whether there were any fingerprints available which assisted the FBI in their investigation is not known. The FBI agents had immediately thrown a cordon, shutting off the canyon and the cabin. They did their own job of fingerprinting the Border Patrol car and parried all questions from newsmen.

In fact, considering the nature of the case, this crime probably takes the record for poor newspaper coverage. The reasons for this will presently be seen.

In order for the FBI to obtain a warrant asking for the right to search the residence of Victor Bono, it was necessary to list the objects they were searching for, and since these included guns and badges of the Border Patrolmen, together with cards of identification, it soon became public knowledge that a search had been made; that while the FBI hadn't found the evidence it wanted, it had found twenty-five pounds of marijuana in Bono's locked garage in back of the house. Then word leaked out that the search was for the two Montoya brothers, as well as for Mationg and Bono.

The two Montoya brothers were apprehended in Mexico. The story is that they had been in San Francisco, had read about the murders and the resulting search in the paper; that they had fled to Phoenix, purchased two motorcycles, driven to a point some sixty miles southwest of Tucson and crossed the border after hauling the motorcycles over the international fence. Then they had driven south to Caborca, then to Santa Ana, through Hermosillo, Guaymas and southeast to Rancho Panzacola.

It was stated in the press that the Montoya brothers talked freely to the arresting officers. Apparently the Montoyas had been driving an army surplus ambulance containing some eight hundred-odd pounds of marijuana; they had crossed the border near Mexicali and were proceeding toward a place in Perris where they were to leave the marijuana when they encountered the Oak Grove roadblock; Bono and Mationg were following some distance behind in a Ford automobile; Bono and Mationg were armed to the teeth.

Sometime around 3 A.M., when the surplus ambulance had been proceeding down the road at Oak Grove, it had been stopped by the two Border Patrolmen, given a casual checking for wetbacks, and the occupants were told to drive on. As the pair had driven away the Border Patrolmen noticed that the springs on the automobile indicated it was carrying a heavy load. So they jumped in one of the cars, drove down to overtake the ambulance and ordered it to stop for a search.

At that point the Ford with Bono and Mationg pulled alongside. The two Border Patrolmen were forced at gunpoint to raise their hands, whereupon they were disarmed by the quartet.

The four smugglers decided that the army ambulance, with its load of marijuana, would proceed to the agreed-upon rendezvous in Perris, and Bono, with Mationg, would "take care" of the Border Patrolmen. One of the Montoyas remained with Bono and Mationg, but he insisted he had no part in shooting the Border Patrolmen.

The police search for Bono and Mationg extended to the Los Angeles area. The FBI was particularly close-mouthed. Getting information from it as to what had happened or what was happening was virtually impossible.

Then the FBI sprang a trap on an apartment where the quarries were supposed to have been holing up.

The raid netted some plates half full of food, giving evidence of a partially consumed meal and indicating that the occupants of the apartment had left in great haste. Presumably the apartment also yielded finger-prints, showing the FBI agents that they were on the right track.

Then, a short time later, another apartment house was

quietly surrounded in the predawn hours. Suddenly a bullhorn carried the startling message, "Bono and Mationg, this place is surrounded. You stand no chance of making a getaway. Come out of the door backwards, with your hands up, and back down the stairs!"

This warning was accompanied by a container of tear gas lobbed through a window into the apartment.

Within a minute or two Bono and Mationg came backing out of the apartment.

The things that followed next are in some ways perfectly incredible.

The attorneys for Bono and Mationg asked for a court order preventing the story of the Montoya brothers from being published, on the ground that this would result in a trial by newspaper and would prejudice the defense of Bono and Mationg.

Apparently the United States Court ordered all officers not to talk to the press, an order enforced by the United States District Attorney's office.

Despite this, certain things leaked out, but the very people who passed the word along in whispered conversations are afraid even now to make any official statement. Newspapers were afraid to publish what they knew.

It is to be remembered that one of the Border Patrolmen had been shot twice, once in the chest and once through the back of the head.

The story is that each of the two smugglers was to "take care" of one man. In this way each of the criminals would be equally involved.

The man who pulled the trigger on the gun which fired the first shot through the officer's chest rejoined his companion, who asked him if he had "taken care" of his man. He replied that he had, and was then interrogated as to where he had shot him.

On telling what had happened he was chewed out. "You stupid so-and-so. He may recover from the wound. Go back and do the job right!"

So the executioner had gone back, put the gun at the back of the wounded, handcuffed agent's head and "done the job right."

Whether this story was the result of a confession made by one of the two men or whether it was a deduction from the fact that the body contained the two wounds is not definitely known—at least as far as any story in the press is concerned.

But if ever there was a case of cold-blooded, premeditated murder in connection with the commission of felonies, where the death penalty should have been invoked, this was the case.

The Montoya brothers walked into court and pleaded guilty to second-degree murder. Following that, Bono and Mationg came into court, pleaded guilty and subsequently were sentenced each to two terms of life imprisonment, to be served consecutively. The two Montoya brothers were each sentenced for thirty years on the charge of second-degree murder.

The United States Attorney asked to make a statement. He was told by the federal judge that he had no authority to make a statement at that time and his request was denied.

The startled citizens of southern California, who had been tremendously shocked by the murders, blinked their eyes. The newspapers, unable to get any more details, let the case die on the vine, so to speak, and these murders have now gone down into the limbo of history.

Occasionally some unofficial statement leaks out, but for the most part the seal of silence which was clamped on the case still remains effective.

Personally, I question the right of a court to impose

such a seal of silence in a case where the facts should be given the widest publicity.

As I have stated before, the one exception to my belief that the death penalty should not be imposed is in a case where police are murdered in the performance of their duty. This is clearly the case in this instance.

If Bono and Mationg escaped this penalty, what good is it to have such a penalty on the books at all?

In this same connection we might consider a case where I made a personal investigation.

A married woman, who, as everyone seems to agree, was a remarkably fine person and ideal mother, sought a divorce from her husband, a big stalwart individual measuring six foot four in his stocking feet.

The woman had reason to be in mortal fear of her husband and she secured a court order forbidding him to call on her or to lay a hand on her. Her husband violated the order and the court issued a citation to bring him in for contempt of court.

Officers tried to serve the warrant but were unable to find the man.

The woman had to keep on working at her job because she had to make a home for the children. Quite naturally she was terrified.

The man, avoiding the officers, went to the house at a time when he knew the children would be in school and the wife at work, concealed himself in a closet and bided his time.

What happened sounds like a nightmare.

I have in my possession a tape-recorded interview between that man and a deputy district attorney. The man tells his story in a matter-of-fact manner which is more characteristic of a hunter shooting a rabbit than that of a human being lying in wait for a helpless woman.

He tells how he concealed himself in the closet, how the boys came home from school.

It was Valentine's Day and the youngest boy had a valentine with a dollar in it. He was inclined to talk to himself; he was never one to save money, but he looked at the valentine and the money and said, "This is one dollar I'm going to save."

The man sat there and listened to the activities of the family until his wife returned home about five-thirty. Then he listened to her anxiously telephone to see if the officers had been able to serve the warrant. When she found they hadn't she tried putting some straight-backed chairs against the doorknobs to prop the closed doors.

Two officers came to "check up" while the man was still concealed on the shelf in the closet. The man heard all their conversation.

After they had gone and when another boy had come home from school, the wife decided to get the family out of there; the man heard her instructions to the children.

Here is a part of what he had to tell the district attorney:

"Well, let's see, that was the last phone call. Well, she started telling the boys, 'Let's hurry up and get out of here.' And, well, I thought, it's time to get down, so I got down."

Q: "Did you jump down from up above?"

A: "Yeah."

Q: "Did you make any noise as you jumped down?"

A: "Sure, a lot of noise. I fell down . . . slick floor and stocking feet."

Q: "And did she [your wife] see you coming?"

A: "Uh-huh."

Q: "Did you say anything at that time?"

A: "Yes, I said, I believe I said, 'You're dead now! . . .'"

Q: "And did you knock your wife to the floor or push . . . ?"

A: "I believe the door did, but I might have done it. I reckon I might have got my hands around her throat."

Q: "Did you strangle her a little bit at that time?"

A: "Uh-huh."

Q: "Then did you grab her by the hair and drag her back through the boys' room to the kitchen?"

A: "That's right. That's right. I kept telling her, 'I heard you tell.' "

Q: "And then did you drag her through the kitchen?"

A: "Uh-huh."

Q: "And you got the butcher knife there?"

A: "That's right."

Q: "And was she fighting back or screaming at that time?"

A: "Yes."

Q: "Both?"

A: "Yes."

Q: "And where was the butcher knife?"

A: "It was in a drawer."

Q: "And in the kitchen, is that right?"

A: "Uh-huh."

Q: "Then was she still on the floor?"

A: "No, she was standing up."

Q: "Then did she run back into that little hall?"

A: "No, I hit her once in the kitchen, right there in the back."

Q: "You stabbed her first in the back in the kitchen?"

A: "Uh-huh, when she was bending over."

Q: "How far did the knife go in, do you remember?"

A: "Not all the way."

Q: "About five or six inches?"

A: "Uh-huh."

Q: "And then did she run out into that little alcove?"

A: "Yes, that's when I got her again."

Q: "Did she have her back to the wall?"

A: "Yes."

Q: "Was she screaming at that time?"

A: "Only to the boys to call the police."

Q: "And did you then have the knife in your hand?"

A: "Yes, in my right hand, I believe."

Q: "In your right hand, you had a hold of the handle with the blade pointing out?"

A: "Yes."

Q: "From your thumb and forefinger?"

A: "Yes."

Q: "And where did you strike her the second time?"

A: "Right here."

Q: "That is, right between her breast and the center of her chest?"

A: "Yes."

Q: "Did the knife go all the way in?"

A: "Yes."

Q: "Clear to the hilt that time?"

A: "I'm pretty sure it did."

Q: "And did it go in hard or did it slip in easily?"

A: "Easy."

Q: "And then did you pull the knife back out?"

A: "Yes."

Now, this murder was committed right in front of one of the children. I have a tape recording of his version of what happened as he told it between hysterical sobs.

Apparently the woman died with her eyes open. The boy said, "There was blood all over the kitchen and—Mommy just kept looking at me and looking at me and looking at me after she was dead."

Now it is difficult to imagine a more open-and-shut murder case than this. Not only that, but the tone of voice in which the man told his story belied any indication of remorse. The traumatic shock which must have been experienced by the twelve-year-old boy, who was forced to watch the murder of his mother, was itself a factor in the case.

The sobbing, choking voice of the young boy as he tells of his "Mommy" looking at him after she was dead is indicative of the shock that this young lad received—a shock that will never be eradicated by the passing of time.

What happened to the man?

It was murder. It was done with premeditation. It was done while lying in wait. It was deliberate. It was murder with malice.

The man drew a life sentence.

Now compare the above cases with the one that follows.

This is the case of a young man who staged the holdup of a liquor store. It happened that there was an off-duty officer in the store at the time. He was not in uniform, but was dressed as a civilian. This officer drew a gun and took a snap shot at the holdup man, and the holdup man instinctively shot back and killed the officer.

This young man has been tried, has been found guilty of first-degree murder, which is certainly the legal definition of the crime according to the letter of the law, has been sentenced to death and is now awaiting execution.

In the Border Patrol case we had professional criminals who deliberately abducted officers in uniform after getting the drop on them, took them to an isolated cabin, handcuffed them to an iron stove, and then went about executing them in the most heartless manner imaginable.

What was the determining factor which caused the court to impose only a life sentence on these men?

According to the press, the judge imposed the sentences of life imprisonment after hearing an "impassioned plea" from the attorneys for Mationg, asking that the slayers' lives be spared.

Furthermore, Bono's lawyer is supposed to have said, "He has a true feeling of remorse for what he did. To execute this particular man would not be a deterrent; it would be a senseless act." Bono and Mationg said nothing.

So we have a situation where hardened criminals who killed on-duty police get life, another case where a brutal wife murderer escapes the death penalty, and a third instance where a holdup man shoots on impulse and is sentenced to death.

Do we want the death penalty or don't we?

Almost from the start of civilization the general idea was that punishment of a criminal would act as a deterrent to potential criminals and somehow enable society to "get even" with the lawbreaker being punished.

These punishments were made so severe that they furnished a horrible example.

When a farmer was sentenced to be hanged for stealing a horse, he protested to the court which pronounced the sentence that it seemed unduly harsh to hang a farmer for the stealing of one horse.

The judge snapped, "You are not being hanged for the stealing of a horse. You are being hanged so that horses may not be stolen."

But does it work that way?

It is a moot question whether or not capital punishment acts as a deterrent on murder.

States which have abolished the death penalty seem to encounter no sudden rise in murder cases. That great penologist and humanitarian, Clinton Duffy, made it a point to ask the people in death row whether they had given any thought to the death penalty before they committed their crimes. His answers were uniformly in the negative.

Of course, persons who have already committed murder and are awaiting execution could be expected to answer the question in that way. I myself, however, have made a point of talking with *potential* murderers as to their attitude toward the death penalty.

So far I have found only one man who stated that the thought of the death penalty deterred him from committing a murder. This man was living in Texas, where his mother-in-law also lived. He hated her with a deep and abiding passion and knew that if he stayed there he was going to kill her. He also knew that state had capital punishment for murderers, so the man moved out of Texas, went to another state and was incarcerated for another crime when I interviewed him in prison.

If we had a uniform series of rules in death-penalty cases, so that the person who committed an atrocious murder could realize he was facing the death penalty, the situation might be different.

However, as we have observed in the three cases just discussed, the trouble is that the death penalty is one huge lottery.

Crimes must certainly be punished, but one thing is usually certain. Punishment without some constructive program of rehabilitation is simply courting disaster.

If a man is given a sentence, put in prison, and then left there to rot, being returned to society after so many sheets have been torn off the calendar at the end of each month, the detrimental influences of prison life will have left their mark and society has just robbed Peter to pay Paul.

Where men can be interested in a constructive program of self-development, a prison sentence may do a great deal of good, but the idea that punishment in and of itself is going to cure crime is a complete fallacy. Furthermore, the idea that the death penalty, as a form of punishment, stops crime is highly questionable.

For hundreds of years we have been acting on these theories, yet crime is constantly on the increase.

Texas, which has retained the death penalty, had a murder committed on the average of every seven hours during 1968. It had a major crime committed on an average of every one and one-half minutes.

Bear in mind that this is only in one state, the state of Texas, where figures on crime have just been released by the Texas Police Association.

9 The Truth Detector

REGARDLESS of how one may feel about the relatively recent decisions of the Supreme Court, the fact remains that the police have been greatly handicapped in their work by these rulings.

For instance, the Supreme Court has decided that the very minute an investigation ceases to be general and one individual begins to stand out as a suspect it is necessary for the police to go to that suspect to tell him that he is being considered as the criminal and then to advise him of his rights—and before any such suspect can make any statement to the police in regard to guilt he has to be advised of his rights.

In brief, the police have to advise the man that he doesn't need to make any statement at all, that any statement he does make can be used against him; that he is entitled to have an attorney present at all stages of the proceedings, including the interrogations by the police and at the lineup—in fact, at *all* stages of the investigation.

The suspect further has to be advised that in the event he doesn't have an attorney the state will furnish him an attorney without cost to him.

Now, quite apparently from a police standpoint, this puts the police at a tremendous disadvantage.

By another decision, the right of the police to search premises has been drastically curtailed.

It has long been assumed that when the police make an arrest they can search the house of the suspect for contraband. Now they can search only the immediate vicinity of the suspect.

The police are adjusting themselves to these new rules. They are looking more and more to scientific investigation. Laboratories for research on criminal evidence are being better equipped and new ones are springing up.

Among the new methods being used, the polygraph, or so-called lie detector, is being brought into more active use by the police. The polygraph is one of the most misunderstood pieces of equipment in the whole investigative field.

There is really no such thing as a "lie detector."

Some enterprising reporter put that tag on the polygraph and the appellation stuck because it appealed to the public imagination.

Actually a more accurate name would have been the "truth detector."

The polygraph is a very sentitive instrument which registers certain human emotions of which the subject may be completely unconscious.

Human emotions are accompanied by physical reactions. We don't know exactly why this is so.

For instance, a good comic actor can tell a joke which will bring a roar of laughter from the audience.

What is laughter?

When we are particularly amused at something we throw back our heads and emit a series of cackling noises.

When a man hears something which makes him sad,

his mouth tends to droop at the corners and, if he is sentimental, his eyes begin to water.

When a person is doing something which requires a great deal of determination he unconsciously grits his teeth.

All these emotions are more easily provoked in some people than in others.

If a man tells a falsehood, the body sets up certain automatic defense mechanisms against detection. These defense mechanisms are usually manifested in increased blood pressure and sometimes are accompanied by a change in pulse and respiration. They are part of the subconscious functioning of bodily reactions.

When we tell the truth, the body sets up no defense mechanism because none is needed.

How does one go about determining whether an emotional disturbance is due to the fact that the subject is telling a falsehood or to some other reason?

It is not at all easy.

The polygraph is an instrument which can and does register an emotional disturbance which the subject may or may not realize. If that emotional disturbance is repeated every time certain questions are asked, the examiner is justified in believing that the questions provoked the emotional disturbance.

But why?

Sometimes it is because of a guilt complex. Sometimes it is due to other matters which have brought about a certain association of ideas.

The examiner must be sufficiently skillful to separate the wheat from the chaff.

This sounds like an almost impossible job, but the really skilled examiner has a lot of weapons at his command.

The ordinary polygraph examination sounds so simple

that most people laugh at it. Questions which seem absolutely inane are sprinkled in with the significant questions.

The examiner may well start out by asking:

"Is your first name John?"

"Are you in Chicago now?"

"Did you have breakfast this morning?"

Then will come a significant question: "Do you know who killed John Doe?"

The questions asked by a really skilled examiner are very few in number, but they are carefully arranged and carefully chosen. A great deal of planning goes into the pattern of interrogation and the composition of about ten questions which the examiner is going to ask.

After the first run of questions the examiner will say to the subject: "Now, I am going to ask these same questions over again in exactly the same order."

This time the subject is familiar with the questions and knows the order in which they are going to be asked. When he is asked if his first name is John, if he is in Chicago, if he had breakfast that morning, he knows that the next question is going to be one which is highly significant, to wit, "Do you know who killed John Doe?"

If the subject is guilty and is what is known as a good responder, he will answer the first question, "Is your first name John?" with no response whatever. But, when it comes to the second question, and the third question, he will be thinking about that deadly fourth question which he feels will represent an attempt on the part of the examiner to catch him unawares. He will, therefore, begin subconsciously to steel himself against a betrayal, and the graph of his examination will show a steadily mounting tension.

Similarly some examiners, after eight or nine questions, will say, "That is all I am going to ask you about the crime, but I do want to know one or two other facts."

The question won't be worded in exactly this way, but the subject will be given to understand that after question number ten, for instance, which may be a highly significant question, there will be no more significant questions in the examination.

The guilty person will subconsciously heave a sigh of relief. He has passed the ordeal for the second time. Now there is nothing more in the forthcoming questions to worry about. Therefore, all the subject's tensions will go down.

The subject is quite frequently intensely nervous. He is being called on to take a test which may determine his guilt or innocence. If he is guilty, he is naturally inclined to be nervous. But if he is innocent, he may be nervous for fear that the examiner will get the wrong impression.

It is, therefore, necessary for the examiner to put the man at ease in order to determine what his normal reactions are.

For instance, when I was in the Bahamas covering the trial of Alfred DeMarigny, who was suspected of murdering his father-in-law, Sir Harry Oakes, the late Leonarde Keeler, conceded to be one of the greatest polygraph examiners of all time, was there to give Alfred DeMarigny a polygraph test.

While Keeler was waiting around, and because newspaper reporters were curious about the polygraph, which at that time was more or less in its infancy, Keeler gave a few exhibitions.

He would, for instance, tell a reporter, "I will tell you exactly how old you are."

Keeler would then start giving a run of figures which would cover a ten-year period, reciting the figures in a monotone, "Forty-five—forty-six—forty-seven—forty-eight—forty-nine—fifty . . ."

Keeler was using what is known as the peak-of-tension technique. If the man was forty-nine years old and had made up his mind to beat the test, as Keeler approached the figure of forty-nine there would be a gradual increase in tension on the part of the subject.

Once Keeler had passed the figure of forty-nine, however, the man would know that he was then safe from discovery so he would "let down."

Keeler would study the graph which showed the gradual increase in tension until the figure forty-nine had been reached, and then the lowering in tension, and he would tell the newspaper reporter, "You're forty-nine years old."

This was a startling demonstration to most of the reporters. There was, however, one veteran reporter who just didn't give a damn one way or the other, and there was no peak of tension evident on his chart. Keeler couldn't tell him how old he was.

This man did quite a bit of boasting. Nobody was going to read his mind with any little black box.

Finally Keeler got tired of it and said to one of the fellows, "Here, here's five dollars. Bet him five dollars that he can't do it again."

So the associate offered to bet the reporter five dollars that he couldn't beat the polygraph for the second time.

The reporter didn't want to take the man's money. It was a cinch. He'd already demonstrated that he could "beat the machine." He wanted to give the man a break, but the fellow insisted. So the five-dollar bet was made.

Once more Keeler ran through the questions. "You are fifty-one—fifty-two—fifty-three—fifty-four—fifty-five—fifty-six—fifty-seven . . ."

Then Keeler said, "You are fifty-six years old."

This hit it right on the nose. The man lost the five-dollar bet.

He couldn't understand how this had happened.

To Keeler the answer was simple. When he had been simply asking questions about how old the man was, the reporter, not caring one way or the other whether Keeler was able to pinpoint his age, didn't exhibit any peak of tension. But the minute five dollars was bet on it and the man wanted to be sure to win the five-dollar bet, he had enough interest so that his tension began to mount as Keeler approached the critical figure and then lessened as that figure was passed.

Of course, one of the great values of the polygraph is that the examiner frequently obtains confessions as a result of the examination.

A polygraph examination scientifically conducted is very, very accurate.

To begin with, the examiner will show five or six playing cards, face down. He will ask the subject to look at one of those cards and not let him know what it is, but to deny having turned over the card no matter what question is asked.

For instance, if the man turns over the seven of spades, he will be asked to lie and reply, "No," when the examiner asks him, "Did you turn over the seven of spades?"

The examiner will then start a series of questions naming the cards that were in the group, asking the subject in rotation whether he turned over that card, and the subject will lie to him, saying, "No," to each card.

When he is finished the examiner will not only name the card that the subject turned over but he will show the subject on the graph the manner in which his blood pressure, respiration, and skin resistance varied when he falsely stated that he hadn't turned over the seven of spades.

Then the examiner will talk with the man until he gains his confidence.

These examiners are not just any old Tom, Dick and Harry who understand how to read a polygraph. They are skilled psychologists who have had a wealth of experience in this field. They understand human nature, and the depth of their understanding is at times uncanny.

Quite frequently their probing questions, their sympathetic understanding are such that the subject realizes he doesn't stand a chance when he takes a polygraph examination, so he figuratively throws up his hands and confesses to the crime before he is ever hooked onto the polygraph.

Skilled polygraph examiners obtain just about as many confessions from subjects before they are put on the polygraph as they do afterward.

This is so because of their knowledge of human nature, because their very questions indicate that they are getting close to the truth, and because the card test and other demonstrations that have been made convince the subject that he doesn't stand one chance in a thousand of "beating the box."

A good polygraph examiner doesn't want anyone in the room with him when he gives an examination.

The faintest noise, the faintest interruption which will distract the attention of the subject can throw off the delicate balance of the test.

However, when the polygraph was, so to speak, in its infancy, I was privileged to sit in on a few examinations, on the strength of my promise to make no move, to utter no sound, and, of course, with the consent of the subject.

I remember one occasion very clearly when the examiner droned out a series of questions which were asked in an ordinary conversational tone of voice, as though the examiner had not the slightest interest in the answers, yet which caused the subject to twist and squirm, to perspire, and finally to break down completely.

"Did you ever embezzle money from the firm for which you are working?" the examiner asked.

The pens showed that the man was lying when he said, "No."

"Did you embezzle more than one hundred dollars?" the examiner asked conversationally. Then after a denial and a brief interval, "Did you embezzle more than two hundred dollars?" This was followed by the question, "Did you embezzle more than three hundred dollars?"

After the examiner had satisfied himself on that point, he asked the following question: "Did you embezzle money on more than one occasion? . . . Did you embezzle money in the summer? . . . Did you embezzle money in the fall? . . . Did you embezzle money in the winter? . . . Did you embezzle money in the spring?"

It turned out the man had embezzled seven hundred and sixty-five dollars during the Christmas season of the previous year.

It wasn't at all necessary to look at the response of the pens on the graph in order to know the truth. Watching this man's chest heaving with his labored breathing, watching the expression of panic on his face, I could have told just about the amount and just about the time when the money had been embezzled without regard to any of the graphs made by the machine.

There is nothing in the questioning of a polygraph examiner that bears the slightest resemblance to questioning by the average police officer.

The police officer or prosecutor will make his questions somewhat in the form of an accusation. He is inclined to say, "Now, John Doe, we know you committed that murder. What we want to know is why you committed

the murder. What did you have against the victim?"
And so on.

The polygraph examiner first develops rapport with
his subject. He shows that he can literally read the man's
mind by selecting the card the man has turned over. He
shows him on the graph where the man's own responses
betray him. He will say, "Now, this is *your* pulse. This is
your respiration. This is *your* skin resistance. It doesn't
take an expert to read this chart. You can see for yourself that you turned over the seven of spades and your
physiological reactions are telling me just as plain as
words that you turned over the seven of spades."

Then the examiner will say, "Now, look, there's some
doubt as to whether you did certain things. If you did
those things, please don't take this test. I am beginning
to like you and I think you're a pretty good sort of a
guy. I don't want to be the one who lowers the boom on
you. If you're guilty, just forget the idea of a test. Nobody can make you take this test. Just say you've changed
your mind about taking a lie-detector test, get up and
walk out.

"I can tell you right now that you can't lie to me
without the falsehood being detected. I can tell you
right now that if you're guilty I am going to find it out,
and if I find it out I'm duty-bound to report it, so
please, please, *please,* just get up and walk out if you are
guilty."

Then the examiner will start talking conversationally
with the subject. He will tell him that we all make
mistakes, that even the examiner has made mistakes,
that he's done things in his life that he is ashamed of,
that he's done some things he would just as soon nobody
knew about, that he doesn't know just why he did those
things. Looking at it with his normal mind, he wouldn't
think of doing such things, but at the time there was

something, some momentary aberration of the reasoning powers, that caused him to yield to temptation and do these things. The examiner says that he thinks all human beings have those spells.

No matter how nervous the subject may be when he comes to the examiner's office, the examiner can discount all of those nervous reactions so that when he has finished he can tell when there is deception and when there is not deception.

Mind you, I am talking about the really good, really expert, polygraph examiner.

Unfortunately, there are quite a few people who have been given cram courses in polygraph examinations, men who are able to read the fluctuations of the pens so as to know what the graph shows, and who can deal with most of the subjects who come to them, but a relatively large percentage of the subjects are beyond them and they will certify that the polygraph examination was "inconclusive."

The really skillful examiner has very few inconclusive reports.

Sometimes a person is sufficiently calloused or is a sufficiently practiced liar so that telling a lie means absolutely nothing to him. Such a person lies as easily and almost as frequently as he draws his breath.

However, there are numerous tricks in the quiver of the good examiner.

He may even think up an imaginary crime.

He may say to the suspect, "Now, about this property that was taken from locker seventeen in the high school last Thursday. You're supposed to have done that. Did you?"

This will be a purely imaginary crime. The suspect will deny that he took any property from locker seventeen on Thursday afternoon, and, of course, the examiner will know that he is telling the truth.

The examiner will, however, give him a detailed examination as to property taken from locker seventeen, knowing that each answer is the truth.

This gives him a standard of comparison so that when he switches to another locker from which property actually was taken at an earlier date and where there is reason to suspect that the subject took that property, the examiner has a standard to go by.

The modern examiner has learned his responsibilities to society. Unfortunately some of the earlier examiners allowed their curiosity to run away with them. When they had a subject who was a good reactor they were inclined to venture into sidelines which were none of their business, particularly in the field of sex.

These people, simply to satisfy curiosity, would ask a man about his sex habits, pry into personal affairs that had no relation whatever to the subject at hand.

Such tactics brought the polygraph examination into disrepute.

That is why the American Polygraph Association has been organized on a national scale and why it has adopted a code which demands the highest ethical conduct from its members—and the Association is utterly ruthless in banning from its membership people who violate that code of ethics.

While there have been one or two instances where the result of a polygraph examination has been received in court, the general rule is that the examination cannot be introduced in evidence, unless by stipulation, nor can a polygraph examiner be called upon to testify as to whether, in his opinion, a subject told the truth.

While some polygraph enthusiasts would like to see this rule changed, I like it very much the way it is.

There have been quite a few instances where a judge, somewhat baffled by the evidence and unable to determine which of two witnesses was lying, would ask each witness if he was willing to take a polygraph examination and let the court abide by the result.

There is, of course, no obligation on the part of any witness to submit to such an examination.

For the most part, however, the result of the polygraph examination is inadmissible without consent of both sides, and it is improper to show that a witness has refused to take such an examination.

I think this is the way it should be.

A good trial judge becomes pretty much of an expert in telling when a man is lying. A really good trial lawyer can cross-examine a witness and bring out bias, hostility, or downright prevarication to such an extent that the trial judge can draw his own conclusions.

Later on, perhaps, when we have a universal law for licensing polygraph experts, the results of these examinations can be used to assist the judge in an advisory capacity.

The licensing standard should be very high and require intensive training in the field of psychology.

As of this writing nine states have laws for licensing polygraph examiners and have set up a high standard of qualifications as a prerequisite to obtaining a license.

The study of scientific examination with the aid of a polygraph is something which takes a lot of time, thought and experience. A whole book could be written about the polygraph. In fact, my friends, Fred Inbau and John E. Reid, have written several books on the subject.

The scientific examiner doesn't always try to establish guilt or innocence as a direct objective. He may think up questions which will be intended to cause certain emotional reactions which can be compared with other responses and, at the end of the examination, may certify not that the man is innocent or guilty but that, in his opinion, there has been no deception, or that there has been an emotional disturbance in connection with certain significant questions.

What causes these emotional disturbances?

That is where the examiner has to be very skillful and very well trained. He has to be a good psychologist, a wonderful judge of human nature, and he has to have a great depth of understanding so that he can gauge the temperaments of both the innocent and the guilty.

For instance, I know of one case where a man was identified by eyewitnesses as being the perpetrator of a crime of violence. The witnesses were absolutely positive in their identification and the police felt that they had an ironclad case.

The suspect insisted on a polygraph examination, and one of the most highly skilled examiners in the country gave him the test.

Whenever significant questions in connection with the crime were asked the suspect showed a very strong reaction, an emotional disturbance.

Most examiners would simply have certified that the man was emotionally upset in his denial of complicity in the crime, but this examiner became interested in something in the man's manner, something in the sincerity of his denial, something in the manner in which the emotional disturbance manifested itself. So he put his cards on the table. He said to the subject, "Look, whenever I ask these questions you have an emotional disturbance. Now, I am not creating this. This is *your* respiration, this is *your* pulse, it is *your* blood pressure. You can look at this chart and see for yourself. You are what is known as a good reactor. Whenever you have a reaction it manifests itself all too plainly on this chart. Now, do you have any explanation?"

The subject looked at the telltale lines on the graph and then broke down and made a confession. He had had nothing to do with the crime in question, but years ago in another city he had had some guilty knowledge of a similar crime.

After that statement the examiner ran the subject through the test again and again and always had a perfectly clear record. There was no longer any defensive mechanism set up on the significant questions.

So the examiner came to the conclusion the man was telling the truth and that he was innocent of the crime charged.

The police scoffed at the record. They had the man dead to rights. It was an open-and-shut case.

Probably the man would have been convicted, but a few weeks after the polygraph test the man who had actually committed the crime was apprehended and confessed.

But suppose there hadn't been a confession?

This gets back to one of the things which plagues the police more than anything else—the question of mistaken identification.

Remember, it is not the police who make these mistaken identifications. The witnesses do it.

Sometimes the police prod the witnesses into making the identification. Once that happens, heaven knows what the real answer is.

Take, for example, a bank stickup.

Two or three eyewitnesses are completely convinced that they can identify the suspect. The police take them down to headquarters and show them books containing mug shots of persons who are known to have a history of sticking up banks.

Identifying a person from a picture is sometimes quite difficult, and some eyewitnesses can remember a person's face while others can't.

There are also "look-alikes."

Perhaps a witness will pick out two or three photographs as looking "something like" the man who perpetrated the crime. The police will start an investigation. They will find out that John Doe, one of the persons whose photograph the witness picked out, was released from the penitentiary a week before the crime and came to the city where the holdup was committed. John Doe becomes a prime suspect.

In the course of time the police will pick up John Doe and will arrange for a lineup.

Now, what happens immediately before that lineup is of very great significance.

If the witness is given an opportunity to take one more look at the photograph, if the witness is told that the man is an ex-convict who has just been released from the penitentiary and, therefore, being without funds, is very, very apt to have staged the holdup, and if the witness is cautioned not to make a mistake, the witness attends the lineup with the photographic image of John Doe fresh in his mind. Will he confuse the photographic image with what his eyes see at the lineup?

But suppose this influencing of the subconscious thought processes of the witness does not stop here.

Suppose that just before the lineup the witness is permitted to "accidentally" get a glimpse of the suspect handcuffed and being led along a corridor by a police officer.

Then the lineup takes place. John Doe is put in with a group of other individuals, bright lights are turned on, and the witness, sitting in a darkened portion of the room and looking through a transparent shield, is asked to make an identification.

It would take a very strong-minded witness indeed not to pick John Doe out of the lineup as the man who had robbed the bank.

Then we go a step further. John Doe is brought to trial for the crime. Before the witness goes on the stand, the deputy prosecutor has a heart-to-heart talk.

"Now, look, I don't want you to identify this defendant unless you are sure in your own mind. But if you *are* sure in your own mind, I don't want you to let some smart-aleck defense lawyer make a monkey out of you.

"Now, the defense lawyer may take you on cross-examination and ask you so-and-so and such-and-such. He will try to trick you with clever questions. So if you are satisfied John Doe is the man, say so, but if you're not entirely satisfied, tell me right now. I don't want to have this defense attorney sabotage my case, and I don't want to have him make a monkey out of you in front of a jury."

Human nature being what it is, the witness is very apt to take the witness stand absolutely determined that no defense attorney is going to "make a monkey" out of him.

The tragic thing is that this happens day after day throughout the United States, and because of it innocent men go to prison.

Law enforcement gets the blame when it turns out years later that John Doe is in fact innocent, that he has been wrongfully imprisoned for a period of years, and that the crime was actually committed by someone else.

If there has been an attempt to tamper with the memory of the witness, then law enforcement is indeed to blame. But if law enforcement has been scrupulously accurate and has tried only to get the witness to testify to facts of which he is absolutely certain, the blame lies not on the shoulders of law enforcement but on the shoulders of the witnesses.

Perhaps you may question the statement as to the number of miscarriages of justice which occur through this mistaken identification. I can cite cases by the hundreds. Some of them are so bizarre that they challenge human credulity.

For example, there was a case which was publicized some twenty-six years ago in the *Saturday Evening Post* under the title, "I Was Accused of a Sex Crime."

Since so much time has elapsed, and since the case has now been completely resolved, I won't mention names, but the case concerned a businessman driving home from work who was picked up by police for questioning and identified by two young girls as a man who had exposed himself to them.

There was nothing this man could do, no way in which he could prove his own innocence.

But the circumstances that piled up were all but incredible.

The real criminal, the man who had actually exposed himself, read about the case in the press and was troubled with a guilty conscience. At first he telephoned, confessing his guilt, then he wrote a letter.

What happened?

The prosecution produced a handwriting expert who was willing to testify that the letter had been written by the suspect's own daughter in an attempt to clear her father. She had supposedly tried to disguise her handwriting, but the expert was sure that she was the one who had written the letter.

Eventually the real culprit couldn't stand the strain. He was a man with a conscience and he couldn't bear to see some innocent individual pay the price for his crime, so he came forward and confessed.

Now let's take a look at the case of F.T.W., a twenty-year-old individual of exemplary character who lived near a service station which was held up by an armed robber. The service station attendant identified F.T.W. as the culprit.

F.T.W. had friends. They rallied to his defense and he was released on bond.

Then the station was robbed a second time and the attendant insisted the robbery was perpetrated by the same person who had committed the first robbery. The witness was even more positive that this person was F.T.W.

Again the suspect was released on bond, and again, after a while, the same service station was robbed by the same robber and the same attendant insisted that F.T.W. was the man.

This time bond was fixed at such a figure that F.T.W. couldn't possibly make the bail—and it was this that was F.T.W.'s salvation because, while he was still in jail awaiting trial, the service station was robbed for the fourth time. Again the service station attendant was positive that F.T.W. was the man, but since F.T.W. was in prison, it was obvious that he couldn't be the man.

Moreover, luck was with F.T.W. because two policemen in a patrol car managed to catch the real holdup man with the goods. The holdup man turned out to have a certain striking physical resemblance to F.T.W. He admitted to police that he had been guilty of all four holdups.

Quite recently a young man was convicted of three separate robberies on the absolutely positive identification of different eyewitnesses who connected him with each robbery.

He was sent to prison. As it happened, the man who had really committed those three robberies was confined in the same prison. The cellmate of the person who was really guilty found out the true story and eventually persuaded the guilty person to make a complete confession.

What are the police going to do in those cases? The witnesses make an absolutely positive identification.

I have recently investigated such a case. Witnesses insisted there was no chance they could be mistaken. They had seen the man in broad daylight and they knew he was guilty.

The suspect in the case was a young man who had previously been involved in a bank robbery. He had served his time, married, started raising a family and was attending college to get a degree which would enable him to obtain gainful employment.

With the man's record and the witnesses against him, he stood little chance. Certain circumstantial evidence also tended to connect him with the crime. The best he could hope for was a twenty-five-year sentence.

Then, here again, the man who had actually committed the crime and who was, by the way, a rank amateur, couldn't live with his conscience, walked into the police station and gave himself up.

The authorities wouldn't accept this man's story until after a most elaborate investigation proved beyond any question that he was the guilty party.

The startling thing was that there was not the slightest resemblance between the man who had actually committed the crime and the suspect who had been identified by the witnesses.

There is still another class of crime which baffles the police and that is the case of the convict who wants to curry favor with the authorities and, as a result, furnishes the evidence necessary to convict the man the police suspect of committing the crime.

Such was the case in Philadelphia of J.S., who was released from prison after he had served thirteen years for a crime he had not committed.

One of the persons who had been involved in the crime had made a deal with the authorities to accept a lighter sentence in return for identifying J.S. as being involved in the crime. Another witness had also supported the testimony, identifying J.S. as one of the culprits.

After J.S. had been in prison for thirteen years an attorney, retained by the prisoner's seventy-one-year-old mother, finally uncovered the truth and a judge released him with the terse statement, "There's no doubt that this man is innocent."

But what can the police do in a case of that kind?

I have had other personal experiences with similar cases, where inmates, in an attempt to curry favor with the police, have seen to it that the prosecution could get the evidence it wanted in return for favors given to the convicts.

Those things don't usually come to light, but they do exist and inmates will freely admit it if they are talking to someone in whom they have confidence.

There is yet another situation where innocent men can be wrongfully convicted—a situation which is very difficult to correct.

A party will be on a drinking spree. One member of the party will pass out. Then a dispute arises and someone gets either stabbed or shot in a drunken brawl.

The witnesses, who are inebriated but not to the point where they are passing out, get together and decide that the only thing to do is to blame the crime on the man who has passed out.

Such a case was that of H.H., who admitted he was too drunk to remember whether he had fired the .22-caliber shots that took his brother's life on the night of a drinking spree.

His brother's wife had notified the police that the two brothers had been arguing in their cabin and that there was a drunken fight, that she ran outside and then heard two shots fired. So she rushed to a neighbor's house and summoned sheriff's deputies, who found the one brother dead and the other brother in a drunken stupor.

In this case an alert district attorney questioned the dead man's widow repeatedly, and finally the true story came out. She and her husband had had a fight. He had struck her and she had grabbed the gun and shot him twice.

The innocent brother was released.

I personally had experience with a similar crime. There had been a drunken party and one of the men had passed out. There had been a fight, a shooting, and the survivor solemnly swore that the man who had passed out had done the shooting.

This man was convicted and sentenced to life imprisonment.

I became interested in the case and communicated with some of my associates: Dr. LeMoyne Snyder, Alex Lee Gregory, Marshall Houts and Art Bernard, formerly warden of the Nevada State Penitentiary at Carson City. We joined up and made a detailed investigation. The result was that the prisoner was released.

In cases such as these the police usually get the blame. Sometimes they are partially responsible for making the identification "easy," but more often the fault lies with the witnesses, the people who testify in good faith that a certain individual was the man who committed the crime.

The extremes to which the human mind can betray the subtle process of recollection is absolutely bizarre.

I was with Dr. LeMoyne Snyder, of Paradise, California, when he was working on the latest edition of his book, *Homicide Investigation.**

At that time we discussed the case of a young man who had been apprehended and identified as a rapist in a case where apparently he stood no chance in the world.

The assailant had taken the young woman victim, put irons on her wrists and then proceeded to commit his crime with sadistic satisfaction.

The police, attracted by the unusual aspect of the girl being bound with chains, covered stores where such paraphernalia might have been sold to persons who had no legitimate reason for its purchase. The police received a description of such a customer and then made an arrest.

The clerk absolutely identified the suspect as the man who had bought the chains.

This man was taken to the young woman who had been the victim of the rape and she positively identified him as being the culprit.

A short time later it turned out that this man was entirely innocent, had been a victim of a mistaken identification, and the police uncovered the real culprit, who then made a complete confession.

In his book Dr. Snyder sets forth a photograph of the two men standing side by side. The man who was identified by the clerk in the store which sold the shackles and by the woman who had been the victim towers head and shoulder above the squat figure of the man who had been the real culprit.

It is almost impossible to conceive of an instance where

---

* *Homicide Investigation.* C. C Thomas, Publisher, Springfield, Ohio, 1967.

there would have been a greater difference in personal appearance.

What happens in cases where the mistake of the eye-witnesses is never uncovered?

Those people who are innocent victims of the faulty administration of justice are buried alive in penitentiaries, serving time in a hopeless treadmill day after day, week after week, month after month, year after year.

No one listens to their pleas of innocence, and if anyone did, how could he go about establishing their innocence?

That is where the polygraph comes in.

If a man is guilty of crime, there are many ways of determining that guilt, but if a man is innocent and is falsely accused, often the only weapon he has is the polygraph.

It is an established fact that it is incumbent upon the prosecution to prove a man guilty beyond all reasonable doubt.

But once that standard of proof has been met, when a man has been convicted and sent to the penitentiary, the authorities hold that there must be "clear and convincing" evidence of the man's innocence before he can be released.

Clear and convincing to whom?

All too frequently this means clear and convincing to the prosecutor, and prosecutors who have sent a man to prison are notoriously hard to convince that they have participated in a miscarriage of justice.

It has been said by some outstanding authorities that after a man has been incarcerated for many years, a polygraph examination is valueless.

I don't know how extensive these people's experience has been, but, in my own small way, I have seen case after case where men have been imprisoned for years and then a clever examiner has been able to demonstrate deception with the use of the polygraph.

On the other side of the coin, when I have participated in polygraph examinations of men who claimed to have been wrongfully convicted and the polygraph indicated they were telling the truth, I think that in every one of those cases our subsequent investigations showed that the man was innocent.

Personally, I don't want to see the evidence of the polygraph made admissible in court. I recognize the polygraph for what I think it is, one of the greatest investigative tools of modern time.

Nowadays the police are properly using polygraph examinations to narrow the field of investigation, thereby saving time and money.

Sometimes, of course, they want to reinforce their conviction of a person's guilt by getting a record of deception on the polygraph. But for the most part, the police like to use it to keep from chasing down blind alleys.

The polygraph is a deceptive instrument because any person of intelligence can learn how to operate one within a reasonably short period of time.

Learning how to prepare a subject so that he is in the proper mood to become a good subject for the polygraph is something else again. This requires a knowledge of psychology, an encyclopedic understanding of human nature, a great deal of tact and a broad-minded tolerance.

Here the question of adequate time enters the picture.

As I've said earlier, a really good, competent polygraph examiner with years of experience in back of him is quite likely to get almost as many bona-fide confessions of guilt while preparing a subject to take the examination as he will after it is completed and the results made known to the subject.

The more responsible polygraph operators would like

very much to see a licensing system put into effect in more states so that a student of the polygraph technique, with only enough experience to know how the machine is operated, couldn't set himself up as an examiner.

The American Polygraph Association, of which I am an honorary life member, is trying desperately to get high standards in the field, to get state examinations and licensing, and to weed out the incompetent examiners.

More recently it has appointed a committee charged with the duty of reviewing cases where it seems that a defendant has been convicted of murder, is penniless, and where there are some indications that the conviction may have been erroneous.

Active members of this committee, who are all outstanding authorities in the field of scientific examination, have consented to donate their time in connection with such polygraph examinations.

This committee is newly formed, but it has done some outstanding work. The big trouble at the present moment is lack of funds. The members can donate their time and are willing to do that, but they cannot donate the necessary traveling expenses. The profession is not lucrative enough to enable this to be done, and the Association is not in a financial position to make such donations.

We are hoping, at the present time, that an avenue will open up so that the activities of this committee can be financed.

As it is today, however, the polygraph is, in my opinion, one of the most valuable devices we have in the whole field of crime investigation and scientific interrogation.

The increase in crime and the recent decisions of the Supreme Court make it vital that our police use new and more scientific methods of investigation. The polygraph is one such scientific device.

The more the police can make uses of it, the more efficient will be our administration of justice in answering the question, "Innocent or guilty?"

10 Probation and Parole

As LONG as the large majority of people are willing to obey the law, police can handle the far smaller number of lawbreakers.

But when the lawless minority grows too large the whole situation gets out of balance.

A ship which is properly designed with the right ballast can weather almost any storm, rolling and righting itself, but if the ballast shifts or if the ship becomes too top-heavy, it simply rolls and keeps on rolling until it is bottom side up.

This is a crude analogy, but it aptly describes what can happen to society if criminals become just a little more numerous.

Crimes have to be solved by determining the identity of the perpetrator; then the criminal has to be hunted down by the police, arrested, brought to trial, convicted, sentenced by the courts; and then the sentence has to be carried out.

It is no secret that, at the moment, police are over-worked, our courts' calendars are overcrowded and our prisons are filled to overflowing.

There is widespread criticism of the leniency of our parole boards, but the fact remains that, generally speaking, when a hundred new prisoners are forced into our penal institutions the doors have to open so that a hundred old prisoners can go out.

This is a mathematical truism for the parole boards, which the newspapers generally fail to take into consideration when they write headlines like "Parolee on Crime Spree."

When a man has been convicted of a crime or pleads guilty and the court decides to place him on probation, that probation has to be supervised by some authority; some parole officer has to have the probationer make regular reports, and the officer has to check on each report in order to see that it is a true statement.

Here again we run up against a mathematical problem.

How many cases can a parole officer handle efficiently?

As I have frequently pointed out, you can take the best airplane in the world, load it with a proper amount of passengers and mail, and the plane will take off from Los Angeles and arrive in New York only a few hours later. The passengers disembark and the mail is handled efficiently and delivered on schedule.

But add another 50 percent to the load which the plane is to carry and it never leaves the airport in Los Angeles. Not only is the 50 percent overload not delivered in New York, but *none* of the passengers or mail ever gets to New York.

Now, that is generally the case with the parole officer.

If he has a case load which he can handle, he can do a very efficient job, but if more cases are piled on him, his efficiency becomes so greatly impaired that the checking-up process becomes nothing more than mere form.

On the other hand, when officials are not overloaded, probation and parole are two of the most powerful weapons we have in fighting crime.

I don't care how tough a criminal may be, there comes

a time when it is better to take a chance on him with parole than to let him serve out every day of his term.

Let us take a fictitious case and suppose that one John Doe, who has been convicted of several crimes, is serving a ten-year sentence at Folsom Prison in California and is due to be released in eighteen months.

Is it better to have John Doe wait the eighteen months out, then start him down the front steps of Folsom Prison with absolutely no control over whom he sees, what he does, or where he lives? Or is it better to release John Doe on parole under such circumstances that a parole officer can check on where he goes, what he does, with whom he associates, and how long and how well he holds a job?

The answer, of course, is obvious.

But, here again, the parole board is the whipping boy. If John Doe gets into any trouble, the newspapers will invariably refer to him as a "parolee" who has committed another crime. Whereas, if John Doe had been left in prison to serve out his entire sentence, and then had been apprehended committing a crime within two weeks after his release, the newspapers would never have said, at least in headlines, "EX-CONVICT AGAIN ARRESTED."

It costs quite a bit of money to keep a convict confined in a penitentiary. Moreover, while a convict is in the penitentiary his family is going to be on relief.

If that man can be legitimately placed on parole after a part of his sentence has been served, he can again become a useful member of society instead of a deadweight on the taxpayers. The same is doubly true in regard to probation. But if parole and probation officers are hopelessly handicapped by overwork from the start, society will be the ultimate loser.

In other words, it is a lot better to pay for an adequate number of parole and probation officers, to see that they are not handicapped by carrying too great a case load, and to make an intelligent application of parole and probation, than it is to build more and bigger prisons.

Parole and probation officers will cost money, less money than keeping men in prison, but money all the same. But as I have frequently said in making talks on law enforcement, "We can't buy good law enforcement in the bargain basement."

11 Young People Can Be Taught to Respect the Law

PUNISHMENT is not a cure for crime. Theoretically, punishment is a deterrent to crime, and undoubtedly it is. How much of a deterrent no one knows.

On the other hand, if there is no punishment, crime is going to run rampant.

When word gets around that police are instructed not to interfere with looting during a riot, stores are going to be stripped bare of merchandise. In fact, a riot or two may be started in order to give looters a good opportunity to do their stuff.

When word gets around that persons who take possession of college buildings, resort to acts of vandalism, desecrate the flag and assault the police with various projectiles are not going to be punished or, if arrested, are going to be given amnesty, we are playing right into the hands of the hardcore dissidents who are deliberately planning to disrupt our higher education, get recruits from the naïve, starry-eyed undergraduates and prevent our colleges from functioning efficiently.

Punishment is not going to cure crime, yet I have known kids who were straightened out by one good paternal spanking.

On the other hand, after kids get older and become accustomed to "getting away with it," even more serious punishment merely toughens them.

In Oregon a life termer bitterly complained to me about the prison system in Canada. He had been released with only ten dollars' "gate money" from a Canadian penitentiary.

It wasn't, he insisted, sufficient for operating capital.

I asked him what he meant by operating capital.

It wasn't enough to buy a rod, he said. (Rod is criminal jargon for a gun.)

In a Nevada penitentiary, a convict, with a record as long as my arm, discussed what he was going to do when he got out. I asked him if he was going straight.

This was one of the men who regarded me as being different from the law-enforcement people with whom he talked. He could put it right on the level with me and he did.

"I'm not going to go whining around asking for jobs," he said. "If I can get a decent job without crawling on my belly, I'll work. If I can't, I'm going to pick a state which hasn't big bitch [criminal jargon for the law providing that the third felony conviction brings an automatic life sentence] and start opening boxes [cracking safes]."

I remember talking with a relatively young man who was confined in one of the state penitentiaries I visited.

This young man's trouble started after his father died and his mother married again. The boy didn't like his stepfather and his stepfather didn't like the boy. That boy "ran away."

He was apprehended, brought back and placed in the custody of his "parents."

This gave his stepfather all the more excuse for petty persecutions and the boy ran away again, was again apprehended and returned, and then ran away for the third time and was placed in a reform school. When he left reform school, he really embarked on a career in crime. By the time I talked with him, he was in a lifer's cell in a state prison.

"When I went to reform school, Mr. Gardner," the man told me, "I knew how to run away and that was all I knew. When I left reform school I knew how to break into a car with the aid of a coat hanger, how to hot-wire the car past the ignition, how to pick a lock and a lot of other information which I promptly proceeded to put to use."

At the present time the sheer number of youthful offenders is such that many courts almost automatically put those who are convicted of a first offense on probation, in charge of their parents.

Quite obviously, the very nature of the case makes it doubtful that parental supervision is going to be adequate, but what are you going to do with these boys and girls? Must they be sent to a penal institution where their criminal knowledge and their disrespect for law will be increased?

Let me tell you the story of Ralph Johnson—the story as I knew it.

Ralph was in charge of a camp for juvenile delinquents. The camp was called Twin Pines. Johnson was very much of a showman. His wife was a wonderful, motherly woman who loved young people.

I went to visit Twin Pines and was completely fascinated by what I saw.

Johnson had designed things so that a kid coming to that camp was swept off his feet, just as I was.

The camp received some pretty tough kids, at least they thought they were tough. When they knew that they were being sent there they had steeled themselves against

any "softening up" process which the camp might have
to offer.

They were completely unprepared for their initial reception or for what followed.

There was a good automobile road from the state
highway into this camp, which was nestled in a beautiful
valley in the high mountain region between the coast
and the desert.

The new arrival never saw this road.

When the officer with the newcomer in charge reached
a certain point he phoned the camp and the reception
committee started out.

Johnson had had a precarious, seemingly dangerous
road bulldozed along the bank high above a canyon floor
—that is, the road looked dangerous; actually it wasn't,
but it has been a long, long time since we have been
accustomed to traveling narrow one-way roads by buckboard. A kid who had been sent up for stealing automobiles had probably never ridden in a buckboard. In
all probability he had never ridden a horse.

He had, however, seen Westerns in the movies and on
television.

When the state car, with the "prisoner," reached the
turnoff in the road, there was Ralph Johnson in a buckboard drawn by a couple of spirited horses, ready to meet
the newcomer, and on each side of the buckboard were
outriders whom the newcomer could readily place as
being young men like himself.

There was an arched gateway over the dirt road and a
sign over the gateway which said, "HOWDY, PARDNER."

Johnson would greet the flabbergasted young man, say,
"Get in," put him in the buckboard, take the whip,
gently touch the horses on the rump, and they were off
in a wild gallop around the curving, twisting, one-way
road, the newcomer sitting on the side of the buckboard

which was over the precipitous drop to the floor of the canyon.

Behind the buckboard came the outriders, also at a gallop.

By the time the young man reached camp his fingers were sore from having gripped the handle on the side of the seat. He was too shaken to remember anything he had planned about resisting the "softening up" process.

From then on the new arrival was kept off balance by finding conditions that he simply hadn't anticipated.

In the first place, the personalities of Johnson and his wife were such that all of the kids looked up to Johnson, respected him, and they loved Mrs. Johnson. Mrs. Johnson took a motherly interest in all of them. Because she was so completely genuine, with nothing phony about her, these tough youngsters gradually opened their hearts to her.

Johnson was a great salesman. He had obtained saddle horses and saddles and other equipment from ranchers and local businessmen. He had milk cows, hogs and beef cattle. He taught the kids ranching. He was also a practical, two-fisted psychologist. He kept a program of building construction going. He taught the kids arithmetic because they had to figure how many square feet of lumber went into a wall or a floor on a building they were constructing. He ran a complete high-school educational course, and by giving them an opportunity to put what they had learned into actual use, he made the young men realize that what they were being taught was practical.

The activities of the camp were on a communal basis.

The camp frequently had visitors for lunch and the boys often put on a program of entertainment with singing groups. Shortly after arrival the camp became a home to each of the youngsters. In fact, the camp became so

much of a home that when a baseball team was organized, and Johnson talked some merchants into donating
uniforms, there was a question on the part of the merchants who made the contribution as to what should be
put on the shirts as a name. Quite obviously it would
have to be something like the Pirates or the Cougars, or
something of that sort, because it would be derogatory to
the dignity of a boy to have the name Twin Pines, which
everyone knew was a reform school, on his uniform.

At least that is what one would assume.

But the boys put the matter to a vote, and the vote was
just about unanimous. They wanted Twin Pines on the
uniforms. Twin Pines was their home. They were proud
of it.

When it came time for a boy to leave Twin Pines nobody said to him, "Your sentence has expired." But
rather they said to him, "On such-and-such a day next
week you graduate."

The graduating exercises were "corny," according to
some standards, but they appealed to the imagination of
a boy. The whole camp turned out to do him honor.
These kids who had been the derelicts of society suddenly found themselves honored and respected citizens
of a new life.

There were simple rules for the day of graduation.
The person who was to graduate took his favorite horse
and saddle and went for a long, long ride over the mountain trails, communing with nature, looking over the
wide, tumbled mass of mountains, the tall pines, the
massive rocks, all of the familiar sights which he was seeing for the last time. Then he returned to camp and had
a talk with Mrs. Johnson. After that he went out to the
parade ground where elaborate ceremonies were enacted,
and, at the last, the "honored graduate" climbed into the
buckboard. The outriders fell into position behind him

and, at a gallop, they went back over the road to the state highway, where the arch over the exit had the words on the exit side, "So LONG, PARDNER."

The record of Twin Pines ranch was phenomenal. I was privileged to see correspondence from some of these graduates who had written back to the Johnsons, just as they would write to their fathers and mothers.

I once accepted a speaking engagement before a club in Los Angeles. I intended to tell them something about crime and crime prevention. Then I was warned that I was talking to one of the most super-sophisticated groups in the whole city. They had heard all of the best speakers. It was hard to capture and hold their attention and they were indifferent to all appeals to emotion.

I changed my plan and took Ralph Johnson there with me as my guest.

When it came time to talk, I talked for about five or ten minutes, telling them something about Ralph and a little about Twin Pines. And then I asked Ralph Johnson if he'd care to say a few words.

Johnson was a self-educated man who understood horses, kids and humans. He had absolutely no delivery, no planned speech, no sophisticated approach. He talked simply and from the heart. And his speech radiated 100 percent sincerity.

This super-sophisticated audience began to sit up and take notice. They started looking at each other and leaning forward in their chairs so as not to miss a word. One of the men began to blow his nose and soon was wiping his eyes.

When Johnson finished, two of the men were sitting there with tears running down their cheeks, and one of them was unashamedly bawling like a baby.

Now, of course, this was an exceptional camp. There

are only a few Ralph Johnsons and Mrs. Johnsons in the world, but I cite them as showing what *can* be done.

Another and quite different solution to the problem of youthful offenders was the original form of "punishment" meted out by my friend, Judge Charles C. Bernstein, of Phoenix, Arizona.

This was seventeen years ago when there were no hippies as we know them today, but rather a group called hot rods.

At that time, in the lettuce fields around Phoenix, high-school kids could work after school and make enough money to buy themselves an automobile which they would then fix up with all sorts of gadgets until it became a hot rod capable of excessive speeds.

They formed a clique, the purpose of which was to "get a cop on your tail" and then "ditch him."

What are you going to do with kids like that?

This was the judge's problem. They were developing an anti-social attitude. The cops were their enemies. Law enforcement was an enemy. The kids swaggered around, arrogant in their independence.

Judge Bernstein got an idea.

He sentenced these youths to ride for three nights a week, four hours a night, with an officer, and to stay with that officer until they had seen two major accidents. After they had seen these accidents their sentence expired.

Of course, the judge picked the cops carefully. They were men who had the ability to bridge the generation gap.

In a short time it was no punishment to ride with the officers. It became a privilege. The arrogant kids became humble apprentice cops and after they had seen a couple of major accidents they learned all too well what excessive speed could do on the highway.

Judge Bernstein put a stop to hot-rod speeding and at

the same time changed the attitude of a lot of youths who were growing up with anti-social ideas.

In the July 13, 1969, issue of *Parade,* John C. Rogers had an article telling of an experiment in Fort Lauderdale, Florida, along somewhat the same lines. Here kids are given the opportunity to ride with the right kind of cops so they can see something of law enforcement at first hand.

· The kids become apprentice cops and soon regard themselves as a part of the law-enforcement program.

One of our troubles is that we are inclined to regard all young dissidents as a homogeneous group.

They are not.

Many youngsters are starry-eyed idealists, and they have enough on their side to give them a series of legitimate grievances.

The point is to help them distinguish between legitimate protest and anarchy so that we do not abandon even a small part of this raw, human material to the life of a hardened criminal.

12 Guns

THERE is an old expression which somehow indicates the subconscious thinking of the American people. It starts out, "There ought to be a law against . . ."

Whenever the American people want to stop something they want a law prohibiting the thing they want stopped, as if laws in themselves were a solution.

They wanted to stop the traffic in alcohol, so they had a law passed to prohibit it. No one has ever estimated the far-reaching, devastating effects of that law.

Now, we are talking about laws against guns because crimes of violence are committed with guns.

Following the assassination of President Kennedy, the killing of Martin Luther King, and the murder of Senator Robert Kennedy, there was, of course, vast public outrage and resentment resulting in pressure being brought to bear on the legislators to outlaw guns.

There is much logic in what people who wish to abolish guns have to say.

Guns are manufactured as death-dealing weapons. Their purpose is to bring about death, and year after year many of those guns live up to their purpose.

A man in a fit of jealous rage kills his wife and her paramour.

An estranged husband, whose wife files suit for divorce, decides that if he can't have her no one else is going to have her and he kills his wife and commits suicide.

A man who keeps a gun only for his own protection is awakened at night by someone walking through his room. He pulls the gun from under his pillow, fires and kills his own father-in-law.

Another man who keeps a gun only for protection leaves it carefully "concealed" in the bureau drawer. But his youngster, as precocious as most twelve-year-olds, knows where "Daddy keeps his gun," and deciding to play Wyatt Earp, he gets the gun and points it at his eleven-year-old companion.

Bang!

A citizen walks down the street at night. He is held up by armed thugs who take his money and then callously shoot him as they speed away in their automobile.

We can go on multiplying the list almost indefinitely. Many, many people are killed with guns in the United States.

If we could actually abolish all guns except those of the law-enforcement officer, we would save a lot of lives and stop a lot of crime.

We would also be sacrificing the pleasure of hundreds of thousands of hunters, and put out of business various legitimate interests such as many sporting goods stores, hunting lodges, and numerous packers and outfitters.

But we would be saving human lives. And life saving is more important than the things we would be giving up.

The question is, can we abolish guns?

That is a question which merits a lot of practical consideration.

In the first place, we realize that we would have comparatively little difficulty in taking guns away from some 80 or 90 percent of the law-abiding citizens. It would be terribly annoying. The expense would be very, very high, but it could be done.

But the point is that by no conceivable stretch of the imagination can we ever eliminate guns from the hands of the criminal class.

By outlawing guns we can make their smuggling a highly lucrative source of income for organized crime. We can put a premium on the manufacture of homemade guns. And if anyone thinks that homemade guns can't be turned out, I can assure you that I have in my possession a collection which my friend, Jack Hargrave, of the Denver Police Force, picked up in the course of a short period of time several years ago while "frisking" juvenile gangsters.

These guns are good for only one shot at a time, but they are very lethal weapons as far as that one shot is concerned.

I think all of us will agree on reflection that we could never abolish *all* guns, and if we try, the very people from whom we want most to take guns, the criminals, will be the only people left with them.

Then why not require registration of guns? Surely people who have guns should have no objection to registering them.

All right, let's look at it from a practical standpoint. What good is it going to do to register guns, that is, what practical good?

When you register a gun you don't make it any less deadly as a weapon. The householder can still carelessly kill his father-in-law. Junior can still kill his eleven-year-old friend.

But for the sake of argument let's say we're going to register the ninety million or so guns in the United States.

How are we going to register them and what are we

going to do with the data once we have collected it? What is it going to cost in manpower and in money to register these guns?

No one knows for sure.

Proponents of the program say it will be "self-support-ing," that they will charge two dollars for each registra-tion.

There is no such thing as a program which is self-supporting when it comes to taking money from the public, any more than there is any such thing as a "new source of taxation." Taxes are paid by the taxpayer. Whenever the government starts any new activity on any-thing like the scale of gun registration, the public has to pay the price.

Are we going to register guns by the name of the owner, by the make of the gun, by the number of the gun, by the caliber of the gun? If so, are we going to cross-index all of this information so that when the police pick up revolver number so-and-so, made by the Blank Firearms Company, they can immediately turn to a computer and determine who had the gun when it was registered?

Despite high-speed computers, that's going to take a powerful lot of filing, a lot of cross-indexing, a lot of bookkeeping, and a lot of full-time employees.

It is highly unlikely that two dollars per gun will cover the cost.

Or are the police at regular intervals going to go to the house of John Q. Public and say, "Mr. Public, the rec-ords show that you have a gun, manufactured by the Blank Gun Company, number so-and-so. Produce that gun, please, so we can inspect it."

This will take up a lot more time on the part of the police. It will cut down on their mobility. It will be even worse than using the police to keep the campuses open.

The people who want to keep guns in their homes are fearful that registration of their guns will eventually lead to confiscation of them, and they may, or may not, have some foundation for their fears. In fact, some of the proponents of the registration idea freely admit that confiscation is the real purpose of gun registration.

If that is so, then after we get all the guns registered, are we going to pass a law forbidding people to own guns? This would entail consulting the registrations and sending squads of police to the registrants saying, "The records show that you have five guns in this house listed as follows . . . Surrender them, please, and we'll give you a receipt. We are disarming all citizens so as to cut down crime."

Will that cut down crime?

What about the criminal class? What about the dishonest people who haven't registered their guns?

This brings us to another rather interesting aspect of the problem.

Once guns become registered, what is going to happen to those records? Will they be open to the public? Presumably they will have to be.

So along comes Joe Doakes. He is a man who has been released from prison after serving a ten-year term. He has had nothing done to rehabilitate him while he was in prison. He is given only a relatively small amount of money, known to prisoners as "gate money," and a prison suit of clothes. He has also been given transportation back to his home town.

Joe Doakes doesn't know what he is going to do next, but he has made a lot of unsavory friends during his ten years in prison. Some of them are now free too.

Joe Doakes gets into circulation—a few friends, knowing when he was to be released, have slipped him coded messages, telling him where they can be reached.

Joe Doakes tells them that he doesn't know what he is going to do but that he has about come to the conclusion that crime doesn't pay.

His statement is greeted by howls of laughter. "Wake up, Joe! Where have you been? Times have changed. We've got a new racket. Come on in, the water's fine!"

"What's the new racket?"

"Why, simply this, we're selling guns."

"But where do you get the guns?"

"Where do we get them, indeed! Look at this. Here's the list of the householders who have various guns. Here's this house at Twenty-three forty-one Eighth Street. This guy's got five guns. Think of it, five juicy revolvers. He's a sort of a gun nut, a collector. Do you realize that within a three-block area there are twenty-five registered guns right in that district alone?"

So the criminals get in a car and cruise around that district.

The householder and his family go to the movies. They take all the precautions an honest citizen is supposed to take when he is going to be out at night. They leave the lights on in at least three rooms in the house. Then they leave a porch light on so they can easily fit their key to the lock when they come back.

Unfortunately, however, this is during the period of daylight saving time.

When the crooks, cruising around, see a house with the lights on before it is even dusk they recognize an open invitation. It means the family is out and plans to remain out until after dark.

The crooks look at each other and grin. In they go.

Even if the police registration list is not made public, too many people will, of necessity, have access to it. Experience teaches us that when criminals want something of that nature they have little difficulty getting it—if they have money.

The tipster is a parasite of organized crime. More recently, now that crime has become a somewhat personalized affair, the profession of tipster is in the doldrums. In an earlier period when crimes were carefully planned, the tipster flourished. He would give the crooks all the information concerning a place. His share was 10 percent of the take.

The tipster remained in the background, virtually free from detection and immune from prosecution.

With the registration of guns, the tipster could come back into his own. Lists of gun registration could very easily be bootlegged into the hands of the criminals who would be most interested.

In addition, smugglers would prosper greatly.

Guns could be run across the border from Mexico. Guns could be smuggled in on ships from all over the world.

Crates labeled "Parts for Machinery" would have a few cogwheels and bearings on top and layers of revolvers underneath. It would be impossible to open them all for detailed inspection. Remember how easily liquor was run into the country in the twenties. Look at how tons of drugs are smuggled into the country today.

Guns would be the same story. Remember that when there is a big demand for something illegal, crime finds a way to supply it.

All these activities would open up highly profitable sources of criminal activity. There would be the resultant bribery of officials, the organization of gangs, the deterioration of adequate law enforcement, and all the other evils which we encountered during prohibition.

Now if the criminals have guns and the householders don't, where do we stand?

If the householder is disarmed, it will cut down the number of accidents with guns. It will probably cut down the number of unpremeditated killings because of passion, but what will this do to the person who wants to protect his family and himself against intruders?

I personally have undergone one experience where two burglars broke into the house at night. I was a kid at the time. My older brother and I were in the house alone with my mother. My father was away on a business trip.

Fortunately the burglars became alarmed when they found the house was occupied and made their escape. But, for a ten-year-old boy, it was a devastating experience. For many, many nights I lay awake hour after hour, listening in terror to the sounds of the night, going to sleep only toward morning.

Ever since, I have had a horror of being unarmed and at the mercy of thugs who would break into the house at night.

One of the most interesting facets of the recent hysterical demand for "gun legislation" is the fact that we already have it in virtually every state in the union.

In order to buy a handgun in California it has long been necessary for the prospective purchaser to go to the dealer and fill out an application, giving a lot of information about himself. This application is then forwarded to various law-enforcement agencies which are supposed to check carefully on the character of the prospective purchaser. After a period of waiting, if there is no objection on the part of the law-enforcement agencies, the sale can be made, but the sale is duly registered on permanent records.

In California also there is a recently passed law making it illegal for any person to transport a gun through any municipality if either the gun is loaded or ammunition is conveniently accessible.

In some states it is necessary to have an identification card which a gun owner must carry with him in order to show that he is legally entitled to own a gun.

In California it is illegal for an alien to have a gun and it is illegal for a person who has been convicted of a felony to have a gun. These rules are pretty much universal throughout the various states.

It is to be noted that in the assassination of Senator Robert Kennedy the killer violated a whole handful of anti-gun laws—but this didn't prevent the killing.

Now comes a new federal law which is supposed to be the last word. The general idea is as follows:

1. Guns may no longer he sold by mail.
2. Guns may no longer be sold across state lines.
3. No one under the age of eighteen years may purchase a gun.
4. No one under the age of twenty-one years may purchase a handgun.
5. No gun may be sold to a whole category of people including people with prison records, proven psychological problems, certain handicapped people, etc.
6. Every sale of a gun must be recorded on a special form. (In effect, this is registration for all *new* guns.)
7. All new guns must have serial numbers stamped on them by the manufacturers.
8. Restrictions are placed on the sale of all ammunition for guns.

This is very fine legislation in theory, but what happens in practice?

The Daily Enterprise, a newspaper of Riverside, California, decided to find out just what the law actually meant and how it was being enforced. Calls were made to ten different post offices, asking whether an individual could mail a new hunting rifle across a state line.

In the post office at Riverside, officials stated that rifles and shotguns could be sent through the mail without restriction as long as they were marked "Firearms" in one-inch-high letters on the package. The post office, in turn, is required to notify local law-enforcement officials whenever anyone receives a rifle or shotgun by mail.

The San Bernardino Post Office announced that it was illegal to send rifles, pistols, or shotguns through the mail except to a dealer.

The Indio Post Office believed that no rifles are mailable except from dealer to dealer, but if you break down firearms into pieces you can mail the separate pieces so that the firearm can be assembled after it reaches its destination.

Another post office announced that a rifle can be mailed if it cannot be broken down into sections shorter than twenty-six inches, but it must be marked and unloaded.

Still another post office said rifles can be mailed if they are marked "Firearms" on the package in two-inch-high letters and the bolt is not put in the chamber.

And so on down the line with varying opinions from varying post offices.

The newspaper stated that a check by Congressman John V. Tunney's office with the Post Office Department in Washington, D.C., concerning the provisions of the new law brought this response from one top Postal Department official: "Well, the Treasury Department is supposed to enforce that law, isn't it?"

An inquiry also brought a frank admission from one of the Post Office Department heads in Washington, namely, "There is a lot of confusion about enforcement of the laws on firearms."

Enforcement of the law is divided between the Post Office Department and the Alcohol, Tobacco Tax and Firearms Division of the Treasury Department.

Then comes a legislative *reductio ad absurdum,* a report by the National Commission on the causes and prevention of violence.

This Commission estimates that there are twenty-four million handguns owned by private citizens in the United States. It advocates that the various states confiscate these handguns at a price which would approximate five hundred million dollars. If the owners fail to turn in their handguns, the government would prosecute.

The Commission also urged a federal set of standards under which the states would require identification of the owners of an estimated total of thirty-five million rifles and thirty-one million shotguns in the United States.

And what would be the result?

We would have to manufacture and sell handguns to certain classes of people. Police officers would have to have them. Sheriffs and deputy sheriffs would need them. And what about banks, liquor stores and jewelry stores?

Would we disarm all of the targets for criminal activity?

We aren't going to disarm the criminal. We may as well make up our minds to that right at the start. We can try to do it, but the criminal is going to be armed. The man who needs a gun in order to perpetrate a holdup is going to have a gun.

We had one "noble experiment" with prohibition. We were going to keep people from owning liquor.

What happened?

We boosted liquor sales. We gave money to the criminal class. We corrupted law-enforcement officers. We encouraged bootlegging and hijacking. We greatly increased drinking on the part of women. We brought an established underworld into existence which is still flourishing many years after prohibtion was repealed as being unworkable.

In my opinion this type of gun law is just as unworkable. If we couldn't stop people from owning liquor, we can't stop people from owning guns.

The idea of "confiscating" twenty-four million handguns, the idea of placing a value on each one and forcing the citizen to surrender his in return for that money is absurd on the face of it. A gun is private property. Are we going to have twenty-four million condemnation suits in the state courts?

How is such a law going to be enforced? How many stations are going to be set up in which people can turn in their handguns? Who is going to appraise the value of the guns? How is the money which will pay for those guns going to be dispersed? What steps are going to be made to enforce the surrender of the guns at the valuation placed upon them by some appraiser? How much money is all this going to cost? What is going to be done with twenty-four million handguns after we get them?

And if we do all of these things, how much crime is going to be stopped?

Here again we would have to embark upon another "noble experiment."

These methods won't stop crimes of violence.

We will have to curb crime by giving the police more cooperation, more power, more respect.

We will have to curb crimes of violence by making the *carrying* of a concealed weapon a more serious crime. We will have to revise our laws so that police, when given reasonable grounds for search, can "pat" the suspect to see if he is carrying a concealed weapon.

Handguns have a definite place in the house. We are entering upon an era of increased violence and the only remedy that the citizen has lies in increased protection.

Take handguns away from the law-abiding citizen who needs them for his own protection and the lawless element is going to have a field day.

Try to take handguns from the lawless element and bootlegged guns are going to be brought into this country in a surging tide of illegal smuggling. The price of illegal handguns is going to go up. The money is going to go into the hands of the criminal class and we are going to start another round of prohibition foolishness.

I am a citizen who tries to keep a sane perspective on some of the legislation that is promulgated from time to time in fits of hysteria.

I am not part of a "gun lobby."

I keep guns for my own protection.

Once when my automobile was broken down on a dark road in the days when there was little traffic I saved my life by pulling a gun on a man who was coming at me with a knife. I didn't have to shoot. Fortunately my assailant took one look at the gun which was pointed at his midriff and took to his heels.

If I hadn't had that gun in the automobile, my career would have been terminated long before I ever wrote my first story.

A few years ago in the state of Washington, two young men, who had long criminal records, were convicted of a rape-murder and sentenced to be executed.

Because these men were brothers and were rather young and because of other factors, a great popular hue and cry went up that their lives should be saved; that the evidence had been insufficient and that the men might well be innocent.

The governor of the state of Washington found himself in an embarrassing position. Petitions bearing thousands of signatures poured into his office.

The governor asked me to act as chairman of a committee to investigate the case and advise him whether he should grant clemency.

It was one of the most embarrassing duties I ever undertook to perform. I was opposed to the death penalty and the governor knew it, but, in accepting chairmanship of the committee, I had to put aside my personal feelings and agree to advise the governor to the best of my ability, according to the evidence and according to the laws of the state of Washington which the governor had taken an oath to uphold.

Twelve jurors had listened to the evidence and had brought in a verdict of guilty which carried the death penalty.

It was not an agreeable task for those jurors, but they had done their duties as citizens.

The Constitution of the state of Washington gave the governor the power to commute that sentence, but having that power didn't mean the governor was supposed to "second guess" the jury. It meant that the power of executive clemency was to be used only if there was some valid reason, some new facts which could be uncovered.

At the outset, when our committee met with these young men, we laid down certain ground rules.

"You are," we told them, "under sentence of death. We are appointed by the governor to see if there is any ground for clemency. The jurors performed an unpleasant duty in pronouncing the verdict of guilty which carried a death sentence. The governor feels he can act only if there are truly extenuating circumstances or new evidence which would indicate your innocence. We are going to look into the case. We want it definitely understood that if you lie to us deliberately and on a material matter we are going to consider that tantamount to an admission of guilt. Now, do you want to go ahead on that basis?"

They signified that they did.

That investigation took weeks of our time. It resulted not only in catching the young men in repeated falsehoods, but it resulted in uncovering even more evidence indicating their guilt. The committee finally had to report to the governor that it could find no extenuating circumstances which would justify the governor to set aside or modify the verdict of the jury.

The young men were executed.

Shortly after their execution a third brother, who also had a long criminal record, decided to murder me in order to avenge the death of his two brothers. He might have made his decision stick if he had relied on one gun, but he relied on two.

An alert police officer, of Reno, Nevada, spotted the outline of the two guns beneath the man's clothing, halted him for questioning, found that he was armed, found also that he was an ex-convict, and arrested him for the felony possession of guns.

This man went to the penitentiary at Carson City. I had friends in that penitentiary. The criminal made no secret of his intentions. He was going to get out, come to my ranch and murder me. He didn't care what happened to him. He was going to avenge the death of his two brothers.

These threats were duly relayed to me by my friends in the prison.

In the course of time the man was released.

My ranch is out in the country in an isolated spot. I had a photograph of the man who had sworn he was going to kill me. For some weeks I had to keep a gun by my dictating machine where I could reach it the minute anyone walked in the door of my study. Furthermore, I had to rearrange my office so that I could face the door in order to see anyone entering. And I had to have an armed guard at the main house. All these things made it somewhat difficult for me to concentrate on my work.

Then the criminal was killed in a shoot-out with police.

If some of these reformers had had their way, I would have been forced to remain unarmed, a sitting duck for a hardened, desperate criminal who was perfectly willing to sacrifice his own life in order to avenge the death of his brothers.

We will never be able to disarm the criminal class, and since that is true I don't want society to disarm me.

As long as we put the police officers in such a position that the citizen ceases to respect them as the representatives of law and order we are going to have an increase in crime.

Crime on the streets is not only going to increase, but a crime increase is going to make itself manifest even in the home.

Even now the citizen who answers a ring of the doorbell at night and opens the door to see who is there is just plain foolish.

There was the case of a Florida judge and his wife who answered the door at night. The judge found himself looking into the business end of a gun. He and his wife were forced to accompany their abductors to a boat. They were taken out, still in their night clothes, weights attached to them, and they were tossed overboard and drowned just as one would drown a batch of unwanted kittens.

A man in Laguna Beach answered the ring of a doorbell. A personable individual on the threshold asked if he could used the phone because his car had broken down in front of the house.

As soon as the individual gained entrance to the living room he produced a gun and very deliberately went about disrobing both the mother and daughter, then raping each while the helpless husband was forced to look on.

The mother of a gambler, who was supposed to keep a large sum of cash on hand, answered the door at night to find a good-looking woman begging to use the phone. She was invited in. Two men, who had been concealed at the side, crowded through the partially opened door. The mother of the gambler was beaten to a lifeless pulp while the intruders searched for the money.

Unless and until we can get more respect for law, the citizen is not going to be safe either in his home or on the streets.

It is hardly expedient for the citizen to carry a weapon on the street, but he certainly should have a gun in his home and he should be prepared to use that gun if he has to.

All of this doesn't mean that the citizen should answer the doorbell at night with a gun in his hand, but it does mean he should have a safety chain on his door or a port-hole in it so that he can see who is ringing the bell; and under no circumstances should he let any stranger in the house at night.

If a visitor at the door says he is in great difficulty and needs to use the phone, he should be instructed to wait right there on the porch while the householder calls the police to ask for the necessary help.

And while we are on the subject of household protection I well remember the words of wisdom given me by a yeggman many years ago.

At this period the yeggmen were professional criminals who "rode the rods" and made a specialty of living by crimes of violence.

This yeggman told me to get a plain but heavy bolt and put it on the door of my bedroom and never under any circumstances to investigate noises I heard at night.

He had a professional contempt for the massive, heavy-set watchdog which was trained to attack. A padded forearm and a sharp knife took care of that type of dog.

The dogs the crooks were afraid of were the little, hysterical, yapping kind that would bark and run, back and forth under chairs, tables and sofas, always barking, barking, barking.

I remember how I felt when this man told me about the number of times he had been in a house when he had made some slight noise and had heard the creaking of bedsprings upstairs, a woman talking in an alarmed falsetto, a man gruffly reassuring her, but finally consenting to go downstairs to investigate.

The yeggman took it all in his stride. He quietly moved over to one side of the foot of the stairs, crouched and waited.

As the man came hesitantly down the stairs in his bare-footed exploration, the yeggman took his "sap" and made one vicious downward stroke, leaving the householder crumpled and unconscious on the bottom of the steps.

It is a frightening thought that our houses are no longer safe, that we are no longer safe, but the cold, hard facts remain that unless we do something to instill more respect for the police, unless we give the police more mobility and more efficiency, we are going to find crimes against the householder increasing just as we now find crimes on the street increasing to such an extent that the wise citizen keeps off the streets at night whenever possible.

13 Highway Patrol

EVERY DAY there are miles of new freeway being opened up. Every month more and more automobiles are brought into operation. Speed limits have increased and automobiles have been given more acceleration so they can now be driven faster than the average driver can think ahead.

No comments on police work could be complete without making a few observations on the highway patrol.

Here is perhaps where the police have the greatest opportunity to improve their public relations, and it is most certainly the place where they can easily tear their public image to tatters.

To handle law enforcement on the highways it is necessary for an officer to have patience, tact, understanding, keen powers of observation and a great self-control. Moreover, traffic officers are continually in a position of extreme danger, something which very few people take the time or effort to understand.

Today we are killing some fifty thousand citizens a year with automobiles and many untold thousands are being maimed for life or put in the hospital for long periods of time.

I understand that statistics show that about half of

these cases are caused either by out-and-out drunk driving or by persons who have imbibed enough alcohol to affect their judgment.

As I have previously stated, prohibition would be a good thing if we could have it. It would restrict the liberties of a large number of people, but it would also save the lives of a large number of people, including those of the highway patrol.

But we tried to eliminate hard liquor from our civilization, and although it was a most determined effort, or as Herbert Hoover said, "A noble experiment," it was nonetheless a catastrophic failure.

So, if we can't keep liquor from the driver, we have to resort to heroic means to try to keep the driver who has had liquor off the roads.

After a man has been drinking he has no business being on the highway.

The best way we can take care of this is by having more and more traffic officers and by keeping those officers very mobile.

I have, from time to time, ridden with state police who were patrolling the highways. Believe me, the situation looks entirely different when you are behind the wheel of an automobile which you are driving on business or pleasure than when you are patrolling the highway so as to make it safe for all motorists.

The officer who sits in the shade of a tree with a pair of binoculars, waiting to catch the cars who don't come to a full halt at a boulevard stop a couple of hundred yards away, may be turning in a large number of citations which result in a goodly amount of fines, but in my opinion he isn't patrolling the road properly.

On the other hand, the officer who keeps patrolling the road may not turn in as many fines, but he is having a wonderful effect on traffic, and he is probably working a lot harder than his brother who is parked under the shade of a tree.

When a state police car goes purring by, all drivers have a tendency to look at their speedometers, and when a motorist in these days of smoothly riding, powerful cars takes time to look at his speedometer with a critical eye he may be surprised to find how fast he is going.

The thing that is particularly galling to me is to pass an officer parked off the road where he is in an inconspicuous position, watching some tricky boulevard stop, and then after proceeding only a mile or two find I am playing tag with a lane-swapper who is cutting in and out of traffic, trying to get a temporary advantage, or find myself behind someone who is either intoxicated or completely incompetent to drive a car on the highway, or near some driver who starts creeping, creeping, creeping over into the outside lane, then suddenly ducks back to the right-hand side. I wonder why that highway patrolman isn't on the road catching these really dangerous drivers instead of lurking on the side roads. Being of a suspicious nature, I wonder if that highway patrolman may not be trying to make up a quota.

There is probably no single thing which has been more disruptive of police public relations than putting traffic officers on a quota. This means making it a policeman's duty to hand out a definite number of traffic tickets each week as a minimum.

Nor does it do too much good just to drill a traffic officer in keeping his temper, being 100 percent efficient, and learning his role by rote.

I have seen some traffic officers who have been scrupulously polite, but this very politeness was insulting.

This type of officer had been trained in the school of ultimate police efficiency. Apparently it is part of his creed never to get friendly with any motorist he stops, and if he finally yields the point, he yields it with bad grace.

Automobile drivers are human beings and traffic officers are human beings.

I was stopped one time in Honolulu when I was in the wrong, but it wasn't a serious violation.

I was in a right-hand lane. I wanted to make a left-hand turn. I looked behind me and found there was no one in the left-hand lane so I cut across to the left-turn lane just fifty feet or so before the intersection.

It happened that an officer was watching that intersection, and he flagged me down before I had gone more than a hundred yards after making the left-hand turn.

That officer was a real human being. He told me what I had done and I admitted it and told him why I had done it. He explained to me that under the circumstances he wasn't going to give me a ticket but that it was, nevertheless, a dangerous thing to do. He explained that his primary duty on the highway was to save lives.

I will always remember that officer. He was courteous, but official, and made a deep impression. Later on I found that it is a general rule in Honolulu that if an officer stops a motorist for a violation and the motorist doesn't wind up thanking the officer for doing his duty, the officer considers he has botched the job.

In summary, I feel that law enforcement on the highways is one of the major problems society has to face today, and here again I regret to find that, in California, Highway Police are frequently called in to assist local police in connection with our so-called "confrontations."

Let's get more and more highway police. Let's get better highway police. Let's put them on the highway *and keep them there.*

And let's be more uniformly courteous when the car

behind us flashes a blinking red light and we are requested to pull off to the side of the road.

These men are saving lives. It used to be that when my rearview mirror showed a traffic officer coming out of a side road and swinging in behind me I had a certain feeling of resentment. Now I want to get out and shake hands with the guy.

14 Cooperate with Cops

PERSONALLY I am for the minorities.

As a lawyer I fought for the underdog. In later years I spent a lot of time and money helping the unfortunate.

When the minorities talk I want to be among those who are willing to listen.

I am, however, against trying to prove *any* point by the use of violence.

I don't know enough about educational problems to be able to discuss intelligently the problems of the college curriculum.

I own to a suspicion that the attitude of the authorities may be too conservative and that a very great deal is to be said in favor of the dissident students.

When I was in high school many years ago I keenly resented the attitude of the authorities which was to the effect that I *must* study Latin.

I told the faculty that I wanted to become a lawyer. The authorities smiled benevolently and said, "Oh well, then you *must* have four years of Latin."

I hate Latin.

In many respects I was a rebellious student, but when it came to a showdown I was always docile in permitting my judgment to be overshadowed by the judgment of those men who had had more experience in the educational field, men whom I respected for their intellectual attainments.

Heaven knows what form of reasoning actuated these older men whose judgment I respected so much. It was probably simply the force of hallowed precedent.

Anyhow, the verdict was that I must have four years of Latin and I had four years of Latin. It didn't do me any good.

Four years of chemistry would have enabled me to get a background which I could have used in cross-examining witnesses in some lawsuits in which I appeared at a much later date and where my abysmal ignorance of chemistry put me in an embarrassing position.

If the college pupils feel that much of the stuff that is being taught them is obsolete and of little or no value, I am definitely of the opinion that their protests should be heard and considered with an open mind by people who are not irrevocably bound to the established educational order of things by the hoary hand of precedent.

But when college students arm themselves, forcibly take possession of college buildings, submit the administrators to indignities, throw them out of their offices, prevent other students from getting an education by interrupting classes, and all of the things which we have been seeing lately, I am against the methods being used.

Violence may be as typically American as apple pie, as some of the students proclaim, or as typical of the American way of life as the custard pie is of Hollywood, but that doesn't mean I want it smeared all over *my* face by some dissident group of students.

I have spent quite some time working with a Negro friend, helping him with his writing problems. I believe that the Negro has to be given bigger and better opportunities and, at the same time, has to be given the chance to develop himself so he can take advantage of those opportunities. I happen to think we need more Negro multimillionaires, more Negro businessmen, more Negro executives. When I was calling the shots for the Court of Last Resort—so-called—I spent much of my time and quite a bit of my money on behalf of Negroes who had been wrongfully convicted of murder. And we secured their release. But this doesn't mean I condone brutality on the part of black people.

And because I am friendly with the cops as an organization doesn't mean that I condone police brutality.

When an officer is called on to make an arrest he has to assume the initiative and keep it. If force is required, he has to be prepared to use that force—just that much and no more; but the judgment of a man who is confronted by a physical adversary and who has to reach a split-second decision shouldn't be weighed by senior citizens on a pair of scales resting on the dark mahogany desk of a judge's chambers.

I am opposed to confrontations in which a line of police is paired off against a line of dissident students.

It is almost inevitable that under such circumstances the dissident students will start hurling insults, and then start throwing empty soda bottles—all of this the American public is now taking for granted with the blithe assurance that violence is as American as apple pie.

But if the police were the ones who stood up and hurled the soda bottles at the crowd of dissident students, a howl would go up that would shake the foundations of our institutions.

The point I am trying to make is that the police have a definite function in maintaining law and order. If we add more responsibilities than they can cope with, we are undermining the efficiency of the police department.

If we don't give them the citizens' support that they

are entitled to, it isn't going to be long before we will suddenly find ourselves confronted with a situation where we don't have adequate police protection. We are reaching that point now.

I don't know enough about the college situation to trust my own judgment, but I have a very strong suspicion that the whole solution of this problem should be handled without the police. But it can't be handled without police unless the situation is kept on such a level that it doesn't become necessary to call in the police.

If the minority contingent wants to study something about the history of the Negro people, I say let's do it. I would a damn sight rather find out something about the history of the Negro than to sit down and learn that "all Gaul is divided into three parts" by studying a language which I am never going to use after I get out of school.

I am, of course, familiar with the argument that when persuasive methods have been tried, and tried in vain, for a period of years, it becomes necessary to resort to violence in order to get the attention of the public.

This reminds me of the classic story of the professional mule trainer in Missouri who was called on by a farmer to train an obstinate mule.

The trainer came out, walked around the tied-up mule, studying him from every angle, then asked the farmer for a four-foot length of two-by-four.

The trainer grasped this piece of lumber firmly in both hands, approached the mule and struck him a smashing blow between the ears.

The mule wiggled his hears groggily and sank to his knees.

The trainer raised the club and again brought it down with all of his force between the mule's ears. This time the mule simply gave a sigh and rolled over on his side.

The farmer rushed up to the trainer and said, "Good heavens, man, I hired you to train this mule, not to kill him!"

The trainer looked at the farmer and said, "In training a mule, the first thing to do—mind you, the very first thing to do—is to get his attention."

However, the problem of the college curriculum is beyond me. It is in a special field and I think the solution lies in a special means of approach. I am concerned with crime on the streets and with a growing disrespect for all branches of law enforcement.

When the police are forced to stand up while a group of citizens of any age hurls insults, paper bags filled with offal and heavy glass bottles, the inevitable results are going to be a growing lack of respect for all law and law enforcement, with a resulting increase of crime in the streets.

I'm just as anxious as the next man to see an equality of education and opportunity. I think that the habit of many citizens of looking down upon the so-called minorities is simply evidence of inadequate intellectual equipment.

I want the college administrators to solve the problem of the college curriculum, but I want the city streets made safe for the nocturnal pedestrian and I want greater respect for law enforcement.

I think these are some of the most vital problems which confront our country today.

I am completely convinced that we need to open up better channels of communication between students and faculty in our colleges. I don't know enough about the problems involved to comment on them with any degree of accuracy.

But this much I do know. If we are going to have law and order, if we are going to have the city streets made reasonably safe at night, we must have more police, better trained police, greater police mobility and better public cooperation with the police.

We can't do these things by calling on police to "keep the campuses open."

Let dissident students learn that their means of protest have to be kept within the law. Let them know that when they violate the law and become criminals they will be treated as criminals.

Let us also realize that as we add more duties for the police to perform we must add more police to perform those duties. Otherwise we are going to have more and more crime in the streets.

Let us also remember that the police are not "fuzz" and they are not "pigs." They are the thin blue line which furnishes us protection in our homes and in our everyday lives.

There are some police officers who are arrogant and heavy-handed. They shouldn't be on the force. The best way to get rid of them is to replace them with new alert, ambitious young men who are anxious to make a lifetime career out of law enforcement. The best way to get these alert, competent young men to take up law enforcement as a career is to make it a worthwhile profession for an ambitious young man.

Let us remember that somewhere in the depths of our language we have the habit of referring to cops as "peace officers" because the police are supposed to "keep the peace."

Citizens generally should concentrate on this concept of law enforcement. Let's make it easier for our officers to *keep the peace*. And let's give them greater public support and a more sympathetic understanding.